Victorious li

Robert Crawford McQuilkin

Alpha Editions

This edition published in 2024

ISBN : 9789362929600

Design and Setting By
Alpha Editions
www.alphaedis.com
Email - info@alphaedis.com

Contents

FOREWORD

DID you ever go with a very dear friend into some foreign land,—say one of the islands of the sea, like Madeira; and there you and your friend vie with each other in making new discoveries of things beautiful and fresh to both of you: new flowers, fruits, birds, vistas in valleys or mountains? If so, you know something of what it means to explore, with a friend, in the land of Victory in Christ.

It was the new and undiscovered country of the Victorious Life that brought us together, Bob McQuilkin and me. (New and undiscovered to us, that is, but as old as the Day of Pentecost.) We should never have been friends but for Him; we entered, not far apart, the "foreign land" of undreamed riches and delights; and ever since then we have been joyously telling each other of our discoveries, comparing notes, sharing our finds, and together thanking Him who alone is the Promised Land, the Life, and the Victory.

God has greatly blessed me through the discoveries of my friend, as our common Guide, the Holy Spirit, has led him on and on into always new and clearer visions of what belongs, in Christ, to every Christian. I am glad that he is now sharing his findings and his convictions with many, through these studies in the Victorious Life.

As one reads this book, let it be remembered that the Victorious Life is not optional for the Christian who wants God's whole will. It is a simple duty for every Christian to "be filled with the Spirit" (Eph. 5: 18); and being filled with the Spirit means having Victory and all that goes with this.

We think of the New Testament, and rightly, as being God's revelation concerning how men may be saved from the wages of sin. They deserved death penalty, or hell. This is true, but have we realized, as a clear-sighted Bible teacher has pointed out, that a much greater part of the New Testament is devoted to telling Christians how to live after they are saved than how to be saved? Have we asked ourselves why this is so? Have we realized what a sad commentary on the Gospel is the man who claims that Christ has saved him completely from the penalty of his sins, yet in whose life is plainly seen, and habitually, the unbroken power of sin?

This book tells how to be as free from the power of sin as from its penalty. It gives God's own message on *present* salvation: salvation from sin now and here.

What the Victorious Life is; how to make it one's own in practical experience; how it may be not only entered into, but maintained; how it differs in life-and-death ways from false substitutes for Victory,—these and other questions that are perplexing many a burdened and seeking Christian are discussed here and answered out of God's word.

Closest fellowship with Mr. McQuilkin for five years, when we were together daily in editorial work, enables me to know that he has come to his present convictions after exhaustive Bible study, frequent conference with mature and trusted Bible students, and wide reading in the best works, new and old, in this field; but above all, after his rich personal experience, through surrender and faith, of Christ's freely offered power and grace to meet all needs in the believer's life. With thanksgiving to the Captain of our Salvation, who never asks us to win victories for Him, but Who has already won all our victories for us, This book is prayerfully commended in His Name.

CHARLES GALLAUDET TRUMBULL.

A WORD OF EXPLANATION

By the Author

MOST of these "studies" have been published, or are yet to be published, as editorials or articles in *The Sunday School Times*. There has been added an introductory article written particularly for those who may have little acquaintance with the meaning of the Victorious Life.

Each chapter has been prepared as an article complete in itself, but there are three pairs of articles which form closely connected studies. The chapters entitled, "Out of Bondage Into Liberty," and "God's New Spelling for 'Obey'" form one study on the relation of law and grace in the life of the Christian. The two chapters on temptation form one study. The chapter on "How Jesus Lived the Victorious Life" and the one which follows on "Serving with the Mind of Christ" form a connected study on the practical meaning for us of our Lord's humanity.

Whenever use has been made of the writings or messages of others I have endeavored to give full credit, but there should be added here a personal word of special acknowledgment. My own entrance into a new experience in Christ seven years ago came through the message of Charles G. Trumbull, who himself just a year before had found Christ in the new way that transformed his own life and with it the message of *The Sunday School Times*. Following my new experience and this new friendship there was the rare privilege of five years' fellowship with Mr. Trumbull as Associate Editor of *The Sunday School Times*, a work that was surrendered at the call of the Lord to go into foreign missionary service. This being the foundation of these studies on the Victorious Life, it may well be that in addition to the sentences in quotation marks used with or without Mr. Trumbull's name, there are statements and ways of putting things that have come directly or indirectly from this association. This applies particularly to the first article; the others embody more definitely suggested applications that have not been touched upon in other articles or editorials in *The Sunday School Times*. Those familiar with "The Life That Wins," the leaflet that tells Mr. Trumbull's personal experience, will recall the threefold division of the needs in the Christian life,—"fellowship, freedom from sin, fruit bearing,"—which is the division used in the first chapter of these studies.

Many have been eagerly awaiting Mr. Trumbull's own book on the Victorious Life, which will deal with the subject in a comprehensive and connected way. It is hoped that this booklet may prove a helpful supplement to the later work.

Special acknowledgment should be made also to another beloved teacher, Professor Melvin Grove Kyle, for his illuminating suggestions on temptation. While this study of temptation and the outline were begun before taking theological work under Dr. Kyle, its development has been strongly influenced by the rich suggestions that are quoted from Professor Kyle.

The little book goes out with the prayer that whatever errors of statement or of judgment may be discovered, these errors may not bulk so large in the mind of the reader as to shut him out from the glorious blessing of victory in Christ, or if he has learned that secret to keep him from further riches of Grace the Word may have for him. As you read through these chapters will you pray through them also? If you receive a blessing, will you pray that God may use it with other readers, and that He alone may be glorified who is our Victory.

July 20, 1918.

PREFACE TO SECOND EDITION.

By the Author.

THIS revised and enlarged edition of Victorious Life Studies should not go forth without grateful acknowledgment for an abundant answer to the prayer that whatever errors of statement or of judgment might be found they should not hinder the blessing that God intended from these little "studies." There is not alone thanksgiving to the Lord of answered prayer, but to those who shared in the prayer for blessing, and it is hoped that the increasing circle of those who are finding new riches of grace in our sufficient Saviour may continue to ask God's guidance and blessing upon all attempts to put into print the message of victory in Christ.

Changes have been made here and there which affect the use of certain theological expressions which were not accurately used, and which would serve to confuse the truth. While none of these corrections, so far as I know, changes the vital truth that was intended to be expressed, the further study of terms used in Scripture, and terms used theologically that are not in the Scriptures, leads to a conviction that it is helpful to avoid the use of any term the meaning of which is not clear to the one who uses it.

While these studies were not intended as a comprehensive treatment of the subject, it was thought well to take advantage of the call for a second edition by adding two studies, one to consider the relation of the work of the Holy Spirit to the life of victory in Christ, the other to ask what the Scriptures mean by freedom from sin.

After outlining these studies in preparation for this new edition, it was my privilege to be associated in Victorious Life Conferences throughout the country with Dr. A. J. Ramsey, who is now giving his whole time to the work of the Victorious Life Testimony. So far as may be possible in such a word as this I wish to acknowledge the great debt of gratitude I owe to Dr. Ramsey, whose masterly expositions of Romans and First John, and other Scriptures dealing with the sin question, have served to confirm and clarify the glorious truth of God's plan of victory over sin which a direct study of his Word will disclose to every earnest seeker. With a first-hand knowledge of classical and New Testament Greek which ranks with the leading teachers of that language, with an intimate knowledge of the ramifications of all the theological systems as well as the false "faiths," Dr. Ramsey for eighteen years has been studying the Scriptures against the back-ground of an experience of the fulness of the Holy Spirit which transformed his own life and ministry. The result is that from all over the land have come insistent calls that he should put into print some of the results of this study which has given a new Bible to scores of ministers and other Christian workers where the message has been spoken.

Accordingly, Dr. Ramsey is hoping soon to prepare leaflets that will discuss such questions as "What is Sin?" "The Body of Sin: Who has It?" "The Old Man: Who is He?" "The Law of Sin: Who Obeys It?" "The Carnal Mind: What Is It?" "Is Romans Seven Christian?" "Is First John One Eight for Christians?" Others will deal with the conflict of "flesh and Spirit," and the question whether a Christian has two natures, and it is planned later to issue a brief exposition of Romans. The studies in this little volume necessarily deal with some of these questions but as far as possible I have sought to avoid encroaching upon the distinctive contribution that Dr. Ramsey will bring in the careful exegesis of these Scriptures, and the scientific handling of the psychology and ethics that are involved as well as the theology.

To Dr. Ramsey I am indebted for a number of the changes in phraseology, but most of all for the glad confirmation that the truths so self evident in the Scriptures, but so obscured in the writings of men, do rest upon an irrefutable theology, an exegesis of Scripture that cannot be gainsaid. It is this that has given courage to speak plainly on some vital points that need clearing up. And it is a matter for encouragement to every humble student of the Word that without the equipment of a specially gifted mind and a scientific training, it is possible to arrive at both the understanding and experience of the simple plan of salvation from sin.

Shall we also remember as these pages are read that while the Holy Spirit does use human teachers to help us to know His truth, it is our responsibility to make the truth our own by seeing it in the Word for ourselves. Let us have nothing in our experience or our understanding of salvation merely as a result of what any man has said or written regarding the Word of God: let us have a glad original experience of Christ through searching for ourselves whether these things are so.

June 19, 1920.

WHAT IS THE VICTORIOUS LIFE?

ARE you enjoying the Victorious Life?

The Victorious Life is a life of victory over sin. Do you have it?

The Victorious Life is a life of constant fellowship with God. Do you have it?

The Victorious Life is a life of fruit-bearing. Do you have it?

Do you have the peace of God that passeth all understanding? Do you have freedom from worry and discouragement so that you are "anxious in nothing"? Do you have the joy of the Lord, which is independent of feeling, and independent of circumstances? Are you able *in all things* to give thanks?

Have you, shed abroad in your heart, the love that suffers long and is kind, that envies not, that vaunts not itself, is not puffed up, does not behave itself unseemly, seeks not its own, *is not provoked?*

Do you enjoy in actual experience the fruit of the Spirit, in its nine-fold variety: love, joy, peace, long-suffering, kindness, goodness, faithfulness, meekness, self-control? (Gal. 5: 22, 23).

Is prayer a precious reality to you, so that you can come to a living, present Lord to talk over every question that affects your life? Do you know what it is to ask and receive, to abide in him and have his word abide in you so that whatsoever you ask you receive? Do your prayers change things?

Is the Bible to you sweeter than honey and the honeycomb, more to be desired than gold? Do you go each day to the Word and get a direct personal message from the Master to your own soul, to meet the very need of that day?

If this picture of the Spirit-filled Life, as it is given in the Word of God, does not describe the experience you are having, then you do not have the Victorious Life. There is something that the Lord Jesus offers that *you do not have.* You may have some of these things at times, you may have glorious fruit-bearing, you may know the Lord in a vital and real way, but if there is not *complete victory* over sin,—which includes such things as worry, discouragement, lack of love, irritation, pride, jealousy, impatience, covetousness, worldliness, lust,—then you do not have the Victorious Life, and there is an experience in Christ awaiting you which will transform life.

Your lack in these things does not mean, necessarily, that you are not a Christian, a born-again child of God, saved by the blood of Christ: it does mean that you are not using in experience what the Lord Jesus provided for you by his death and resurrection.

The First Step Toward Victory

Do you believe there is something in the Christian life that you have not found, or that you do not possess? And do you want that experience? If you can say yes to these questions, then give thanks to God that he has led you by his Grace to take the first step toward Victory.

The first step toward the Victorious Life is for a Christian to recognize the need, to realize that there is an experience that he does not possess. As in the case of an unconverted man who can never understand nor receive the Gospel message till he comes to the place of seeing himself a sinner, so a satisfied and defeated Christian is in no place to receive the Victorious Life message. The defeated man described in the seventh chapter of Romans cries out, "O wretched man that I am! who shall deliver me out of the body of this death?" The reason some Christians have never tasted the victory of the eighth chapter of Romans is because they have never known anything of the struggle that is described in the seventh chapter of Romans.

A College Student's "Problem"

A young college student came to a speaker on the Victorious Life for an interview, but started in by saying that he had no "problems" in his Christian life.

"Do you have complete victory over sin?"

"Well, it depends on what you mean by sin."

"Do you ever have angry thoughts and feelings in your heart toward others?"

"Do you mean get 'peeved' at people? Sure I do."

"Do you ever worry about things?"

"Worry about things! I should say I do. Everybody does."

"Do you ever have impure thoughts and desires in your heart?"

"Yes, I do."

"These things are sins, aren't they?"

"Yes, I suppose they are."

"These are the things that put the Lord Jesus on the Cross. You have these things in your life, you do not have victory over them and other like sins, and yet you tell me you have no 'problem' in your Christian life."

This young college student was led by the Spirit to see the inner meaning of sin and to confess that he did indeed need something in his Christian life that he did not have.

The sin problem is the problem of all problems. If the sin problem in your life is settled in God's way, you will have the secret of solving all other problems in God's way. Fellowship with God, peace, joy, freedom from anxiety, power for service, the right enjoyment and use of Bible study and prayer, all of these things and every gift of grace will be open to you when you get the sin question settled. At Victorious Life conferences, Christians come to the leaders and say that they are not troubled in the matter of getting victory over sin, but that they do not get results in their Christian service and they want the Holy Spirit for power in service. In every such case it is found that the real difficulty is the sin question: there is not complete, Spirit-given victory over inward sin. When that is settled the power in service and the results follow.

When God came to choose a name for his Son, some one has pointed out, he went to the heart of the subject and called his name "Jesus," because it is he that shall save his people from their sins. It is going to the heart of the Christian's need, then, first to emphasize victory over sin as the road to all other blessings of the Abundant Life.

What is God's way of securing this Victory?

There are two ways of getting money, or any other thing of value—either working for it, or receiving it as a gift.

Two Ways to Seek Victory

There are two ways of seeking after salvation—working for it or receiving it as a gift. But there are not two ways of *obtaining* salvation or eternal life. For when a sinner works, he works sin; and the *wages* of sin is death. Life is never earned. Death is. Life must be given. So the free gift of God, the only author of life, is eternal life. We are saved by Grace, not by works, for the least particle of "works" would make Grace void.

There are two ways of seeking after the Victorious Life, present freedom from the law of sin—working for it, striving and struggling after it, or receiving it as a free gift, without effort. There are not two ways of *obtaining* Victory. For when a saved sinner struggles with inward desires toward evil he is under the law—using his own efforts—and not under grace, and the struggle at some time or other always ends in defeat.

The Victorious Life is a free gift from God. It cannot be earned. It therefore must be accepted on the same terms as salvation from the penalty of sin. It must be received as a gift. To enjoy a gift one has but to take it, and thank the giver.

"Sin shall not have dominion over you: for ye are not under law, but under grace" (Rom. 6:14). "My grace is sufficient for thee" (2 Cor. 12:9).

To believe these words of God is to enjoy the gift of victory.

"The law of the Spirit of life in Christ Jesus made me free from the law of sin and of death" (Rom. 8:2).

To believe this word is to enjoy present freedom from the law of sin. "Every one that committeth sin is the bondservant of sin.... If therefore the Son shall make you free, ye shall be free indeed" (John 8:34, 35).

"If ye are led by the Spirit, ye are not under the law" (Gal. 5:18), that is, we are under Grace. And Grace means, Jesus Christ is doing it all for us, winning the victory for us by his indwelling power.

The Much More Salvation

These Scriptures show clearly that God's way of victory over present sin is by the power of the Holy Spirit. That new law, the law of the Spirit, makes us free from the law of sin. "If, while we were enemies, we were reconciled to God through the death of his Son, much more, being reconciled, shall we be saved by his life" (Rom. 5:10). This is the "much more salvation," present salvation by his indwelling life. Reconciled saints need to be "saved," and the Victorious Life is nothing other than salvation by free grace, in present action, applied to each temptation and problem.

God's plan of salvation from the present power of sin, therefore, is exactly the same plan as he has revealed for salvation from the death penalty of sin. Both are by free grace without effort on your part. Both are to be received and enjoyed by faith. After the remarkable passage in the fifth chapter of Galatians, which gives the nine-fold fruit of the Spirit, there is this statement: "If we live by the Spirit, by the Spirit let us also walk" (Gal. 5:25). That is, since we have been born again by the supernatural power of the Holy Spirit, by that same supernatural Spirit, without effort on our part, let us also live our daily lives, winning victory over sin by just letting the fruit of the Spirit be produced, letting the rivers of living waters flow out (John 7:38).

It follows from this that every Christian really has received the gift of Victory from God, for it is just the indwelling Christ through the power of the Spirit. But how few, how very few Christians are enjoying the remarkable results of that gift, the freedom from the law of sin, the fruit of the Spirit. Why is this? A generation ago there were very many earnest Christians who thought it presumptuous to be sure of their salvation. They may have been saved and been blessed with all spiritual blessings in Christ, but they were not, and some Christians to-day are not, *enjoying assurance of salvation*. Even so defeated Christians, who walk now and then after the flesh and fall into sin, are not enjoying the freedom that Christ purchased for them. They are not living up to their privileges in the Lord. The word of freedom has not been benefiting them, because it has not been united by faith with them that heard. "For indeed we have had good tidings preached unto us, even as also they: but the word of hearing did not profit them, because it was not united by faith with them that heard" (Heb. 4:2).

The Two Simple Conditions

The simplicity of entering into this New Life has been a stumbling block to many. For there are but two conditions for victory, and every Christian has been given grace to meet these two conditions. The first is surrender. For that resurrection life of Jesus can only operate when our self effort ceases. "Yield yourselves unto God" (Rom. 6:13). Or as Weymouth translates it: "Surrender your very selves unto God." And this was spoken to Christians. This surrender of the Christian to God is positive, not negative. It is not as a surrender of things, nor of an evil self life, but a yielding of self with all its powers to God, as alive from the dead. With this positive surrender everything contrary to God's will goes out of the life.

Surrender a Definite Matter

Failure frequently comes in the life of Victory because there has not been a complete surrender. Something has been held back. Or we have been too superficial in our understanding of what crucifixion of the old self life means. Now our Lord is lovingly ready to meet us when we come eager for full salvation and willing to make full surrender to him. He will show us if we ask him, *and wait for his answer*, whether there is anything that is not wholly surrendered to him. Some Christians say this matter of surrender is very vague, and they cannot tell whether they have really surrendered completely. As a matter of fact, the Holy Spirit is always very definite when we deal with him earnestly. One woman who said the surrender matter was entirely too vague for her to know whether she had surrendered, after some questioning remarked: "Well, of course, I would not be willing to have my two sons go to Africa as missionaries." The matter of surrender was very definite for her and until this Christian mother lays her two boys on the altar for Christ she will not know complete victory.

Young people sometimes stumble over surrendering such things as worldly amusements, the theatre, dramatic moving pictures, dancing, card-playing, smoking. They argue that they do not regard these things as sins, though others may believe them to be. But surely if we are facing the question of getting such a great Gift as Christ as our Victory and very Life, these things are small matters to yield. But if they are not sins, are they "weights" in the Christian race? "Let us ... lay aside *every weight*, and the sin which doth so easily beset us" (Heb. 12:1).

When A Christian Robs Christ

But, it may be objected, how can a Christian surrender? Does he not already belong to Christ? Ah, that is the sad tragedy of it. Will a man rob God? Yes, the Church of Christ is largely robbing him to-day of the only offering he cares for—ourselves as living sacrifices. We are indeed bought with a price, the precious blood of Christ, we are not our own, we belong to him. Have *you* acknowledged this ownership in every detail, not with your lips alone, but with your life, in its every action? That is the first requirement for Victory. And Victory will never be enjoyed until the surrender question is settled. An earnest young Christian woman was in defeat and distress because there was something she would not yield. She acknowledged it was pride, but she could not give it up.

"Whom do you belong to?" she was asked.

"Christ."

"What price did he pay for you?"

"His own life."

"But you are saying to him there is something you are holding back. What are you doing?"

"I suppose I am crucifying him afresh," she answered, the tears coming.

"Yes, you are robbing him."

But the struggle went on and she would not yield.

"Will you kneel down and just tell the Lord that you are robbing him, and that you intend to keep on robbing him?"

She shrank from such a thought, and she kneeled down and told her Lord that she *would* yield that one thing she was holding back, and that there was nothing that she was not willing to do that he wanted.

She arose with a radiant face, and as the days went on it developed that God did not want her to do the thing she was shrinking back from doing. A Christian may be kept out of victory because he says he would not be willing to go to the mission field, or send his sons to the mission field. God *may not want him to go*, but he can never have Victory as long as there is an unwillingness to do what God *may* want him to do. For this is doubting God and his love.

More Needed Than Surrender

But there are multitudes of Christians who are truly surrendered, holding nothing back, who do not have Victory. For the surrendered life is not necessarily the Victorious Life. Surrender is *our* part. The supernatural work of Victory is *God's* part. *God is doing his part as soon as we yield ourselves,* and we get the benefit of it when we believe that fact. This is Victory by faith. "Faith does nothing. Faith believes that God is doing it all." Faith is just believing the word of God. Those marvelous promises, or rather "facts" of God's Grace which have been quoted above can only be received by the Christian who is holding nothing back from God. Then all the rest is God's work.

Is he faithful? We have surrendered. Is our part then to believe that God will give us Victory? *No, that is not faith.* "Victory's final secret," as Mr. Trumbull has put it, is to believe that Christ *is* doing his part, that his Grace *is* sufficient, that we *are* free from the law of sin, that we *are* under Grace and not under law and that therefore sin *is not having dominion* over us, that he *is* meeting all our needs, but we *are* walking in the Spirit. This is "letting God."

Will you not "let go, and let God?" Now?

If you do, you can say with Paul, not only as a truth of your position in Christ, but as the blessed truth of your experience: "I have been crucified with Christ; and it is no longer I that live, but Christ liveth in me" (Gal. 2:20).

What It Is Not

The Victorious Life is not a life free from temptation, but a life of victory over temptation. First Corinthians 10:13, with its "there is no temptation" is an absolute guarantee from God that victory over all temptations is possible; for he himself provides the way of escape. Jesus,—in his resurrection Life,— is the Way.

The Victorious Life is not a life free from the possibility of falling into sin. It is always possible at any moment to sin, and as soon as our eyes get off Jesus faith slips, self is in control, and the result is sin.

The Victorious Life is not dependent on circumstances. Nothing is too hard for God, not even your hard circumstances. And let us always remember that the Victorious Life is *"the Life that is Christ."* He is as able under one circumstance as under another.

The Victorious Life is not an attainment by growth. True growth in Grace really begins when we take the Grace of the Lord for complete victory over sin. Growth in Grace does not mean gradually getting rid of our sins, but it does mean growing from one degree of glory to another degree of glory as we behold the Lord and are changed into his image (2 Cor. 3:18).

The Victorious Life gives no cause for boasting of spiritual attainment. Grace excludes boasting. It gives us no holiness of our own. The holiness and the victory are His, and the most mature saint in the walk of faith needs the same secret of Victory as the young Christian just entering into the Life. His strength is ever made perfect in weakness. My weakness is never made stronger, though as I learn more of the Bible teaching of what faith is I may get more and more established in acting by faith.

Continuing in Victory

We continue in the Life of Victory as we entered it, by continuing the attitude of surrender and faith, moment by moment. It is the principle of "contact"; as long as the trolley keeps on the wire the electric power is supplied to run the car; as we keep looking unto Jesus there is Victory. If a slip of faith comes, if the trolley gets off the wire, and sin enters (which is always possible but never necessary), do not stop to argue with Satan about the sin or listen to his suggestion that you never had Victory: confess, receive instant forgiveness (1 John 1:9), look again in faith just as when you entered into the blessed "rest of faith."

Does this message leave you with joy and gladness in your heart, because you know that this life is yours? Have you taken the Gift? Or are you like the young Christian who told an older woman that she had surrendered and believed *a thousand times*, and she was in hopeless darkness about it all.

"Well," this older Christian said, "just stop doing that, or trying to do anything, and trust him to do it all."

"I have done that a hundred times," was the discouraged answer.

She had no will power to do anything, and she was hungry for Victory.

"If you can do nothing else, just lift up your heart to Christ."

"I can't. My heart is too heavy to lift up."

It Is as Simple as This

"Well, one thing you can do, for it is just a physical act. You can lift up your eyes. Will you do that?"

The young woman promised that she would do that, and on the way home she kept her eyes directed upward as unto him. The next day she gave her testimony with a radiant face, rejoicing in the Lord: "I lifted up my eyes, and my heart went up with them."

The Victorious Life is just as gloriously simple as that—just looking up—unto Jesus—and KEEP ON LOOKING.

OUT OF BONDAGE INTO LIBERTY

"THEY do not care a snap of their fingers whether Abraham was justified by faith or works," writes a leading American preacher in a recent article that seeks to interpret the heart-cry of men to-day for a prophet who can give them "a spiritual interpretation of the world-rending and home-smashing events that are taking place."

Yet that very same question which was the all-important thing for Abraham, to-day, nearly four thousand years later, is still the question that goes to the root of the world's spiritual problem.

There is nothing more important for the Christian to understand than the distinction between law and grace. For to understand that is to have in one's heart the Gospel message. It is not too much to say that the chief cause of powerlessness in the Christian church to-day, a powerlessness that is made the more acutely evident by the world's sore travail, is that so many thousands of Christians are still living under law.

They have not found the emancipation of grace.

They do not walk at liberty, which was purchased for us by Christ.

They do not stand fast in the freedom wherewith Christ has set us free.

They are not "free indeed" with the freedom which the Son of God won for us.

This is not an academic question. It is not a discussion of points of law, nor the making of fine distinctions in the deeper spiritual mysteries. *It is a question of sin.*

When our Lord was telling the Jews that if they believed him and followed him they would know the truth, and the truth would set them free, they threw back their shoulders in their pride of ancestry and boasted that they were Abraham's seed, and were never in bondage to any man. The Son of God did not stop to discuss questions of race, or of political liberty, but went to the heart of the matter with one of his tremendous verilies: "Verily, verily, I say unto you, Every one that committeth sin is the bondservant of sin" (John 8:34).

Christians Who Are Bondslaves

That Word of the King of kings is the word that needs to be thundered to-day, or, what is more effective, whispered to-day into the souls of men. There is no bondslavery comparable to this. A man may be on the side of righteousness so far as the conflict of nations is concerned to-day, but what avails that for the solving of his individual problem if he is the bondservant of sin?

If, then, the question of law and grace is a question of sin, it is the most vital matter that can concern men to-day. Always alongside of sin is another word beginning with S—"Salvation,"—that is, this word is always alongside of sin in *this age of Grace*. When our Lord told the Jews of this bondslavery, he did not leave them there, but added that wondrous word: "If therefore the Son shall make you free, ye shall be free indeed."

There is needed to-day a great challenge to be thrown at an unbelieving world, a testimony that cannot be answered,—*Christians walking at liberty*, men and women living in the midst of these awful days of stress with the "freedom indeed" which belongs only to sons of God. But instead of that an unbelieving world is constantly face to face with the puzzling spectacle of professing Christians who are bondservants of sin, who do not know the meaning of liberty.

For let us remember the word of the Master, and not nullify it with theological explanations to make it fit into the experiences of Christians: "Verily, verily, I say unto you, Every one that committeth sin is the bondservant of sin." And Christians are bondservants of sin because they are living under law and not under grace. They are not using, not enjoying, the freedom that Jesus Christ purchased for us.

Have We Nothing to Do with Law?

So fundamental is the correct understanding of the Christian's relation to the law, that if Satan is not able to beguile Christians into staying in bondage under the law he will seek to drive them into an opposite error that is just as deadly to true liberty. This is the notion that a Christian has nothing to do with the law, and is under no obligation to have his life conform to it. Young Christians who have seen something of the wonder of their deliverance from the law have jumped to the conclusion that the Old Testament books that deal with the dispensation of law have such an indirect bearing upon their lives that they can neglect them. Portions of the New Testament are also divided in this fashion from the rest of the Word, and even Christians with a deep spiritual vision have argued that the Sermon on the Mount had little in it for them because it was on legal ground, and we are under grace. Their teachers may not have intended this application of their instruction about freedom from the law, but it illustrates the danger, and shows the need of clear light from the Word to avoid the pitfalls on each side.

So the Word of God urges on the one hand, "For freedom did Christ set us free: stand fast therefore, and be not entangled again in a yoke of bondage" (Gal. 5:1), and cautions on the other, "For so is the will of God, that by well-doing ye should put to silence the ignorance of foolish men: as free, and not using your freedom for a cloak of wickedness, but as bondservants of God" (1 Peter 2:16).

And Paul puts the two messages together in Galatians 5:13 and 14: "For ye, brethren, were called for freedom; only use not your freedom for an occasion to the flesh, but through love be servants one to another. For the whole law is fulfilled in one word, even in this: Thou shalt love thy neighbor as thyself."

Law in the New Testament

But in what sense are we freed from the law, if we are still to keep the law? The New Testament takes hold of the law of God as revealed in the Old, and makes it infinitely higher in its requirements.

Some men say that their Gospel is the Sermon on the Mount.

It is the most hopeless Gospel a sinner ever struggled with.

For in this sermon our Lord pours the spiritual meanings into the law of God. It may have been possible for a man to abstain from the outward act of murder, but our Lord takes that command and shows that the inward fact of murder is in a man's heart if he is angry with his brother. So does the Master lift the command against impurity into a place where the strong moral man, who does not have the secret of victory, is convicted of impurity.

Not only is there this spiritual interpretation of the law, which makes it the more impossible to keep it, but there is the new commandment the Lord gave his disciples, to love one another *as he loved them*. And as though this were not enough, the New Testament epistles, after the death and resurrection, when the dispensation of law was fully over, show us that to break the law of God at one point makes us guilty of all: "Howbeit if ye fulfil the royal law, according to the scripture, Thou shalt love thy neighbor as thyself, ye do well: but if ye have respect of persons, ye commit sin, being convicted by the law as transgressors. For whosoever shall keep the whole law, and yet stumble in one point, he is become guilty of all. For he that said, Do not commit adultery, said also, Do not kill. Now if thou dost not commit adultery, but killest, thou art become a transgressor of the law" (James 2:8-11).

This startling passage says that if Christians have respect of persons—and has not the Spirit here put his finger upon one of the most pathetic and abominable sins of Christian churches of our day?—these Christians are convicted as transgressors of the law, and are guilty of all. Then the Apostle goes on to speak of the sins of murder and adultery as samples of the kind of thing that a Christian is guilty of when he shows respect of persons,—the awful sin of unlove.

Law Never Abrogated

This leads us into the truth that the law of God is pure and holy and spiritual, and has never been abrogated. The New Covenant does not take away the law: it provides a way of fulfilling the law. There are many senses in which the word "law" is used in the Scriptures, but we are looking now at the righteous law of God which must be fulfilled, and the breaking of which is sin, for sin is lawlessness, or the breaking of the law. James tells us that to stumble in one point is to break the whole law, for the law is a unity.

The law is a unity because it is an expression of the character of God, and God is one.

To break it in one point is to sin against God. It is a true revelation of the Scriptures that "God is law," though these words do not occur. The words "God is love" do occur, and love is the fulfilling of the law.

When God gave the perfect law to men God knew that men could not keep it apart from the secret of Grace. *But men did not know it.* And God cannot do anything for a man by grace until man learns that he is a transgressor of the law of God, and that it is *impossible for him to keep it.* Israel said, "All that Jehovah hath spoken we will do." They indeed needed a tutor unto Christ.

The law, then, was added to show man what sin is, to make sin exceeding sinful, to prove to man that he is a sinner. This work the law did all through the old dispensation. But this work the law must continue to do for every individual before he can enter into the meaning of grace.

That Seventh of Romans Struggle

That is what the struggle of the seventh chapter of Romans means. That is a struggle under law, the picture of a man who has been brought under condemnation by the law. The law is a great mirror let down from heaven in which a man may see himself as he is. That is why the law brings condemnation and death. It is a curse,—not because the law is not holy, but because it convicts the man of his unholiness. Law does this in the New Testament as well as the Old, and with infinitely more searching terribleness because of the high spiritual interpretation of the inner meaning of the outward commands. The law of God has done its work in a Christian when he has seen that it is impossible for him to be good according to God's standard.

Not all have seen this. Dr. Scofield tells of a gentleman who came to him at the close of a talk on how a Christian might get out of the struggle of the seventh chapter of Romans into the victory of the eighth chapter, and asked him this: "Doctor, what was the trouble with Paul anyway? Why did he find it so hard to be good? I don't find it very hard to be good."

"What do you mean by being good?" the preacher asked.

"What every one means—living a clean life, being honest, paying your debts, treating people right, and if your neighbor gets in trouble put your hand in your pocket and help him out."

"Oh," Dr. Scofield responded, "Paul did those things all his life. Any *gentleman* would do those things. Paul was not talking of that when he said it was a struggle to be good."

"Well, what did he mean?" the business man asked, somewhat taken aback.

"Not Built That Way!"

"Did you ever try to be meek?" was the preacher's next question.

"What's that?"

"Did you ever try to be meek?"

"No, sir! I don't admire a meek man."

"Don't you? Well, God does. His Son was meek and lowly. But now suppose you started off some morning and determined to be meek all that day, to love everybody, no matter what mean things another man might say. Would you find it easy?"

"I couldn't do it. That's not in my line. I'm not built that way."

Just so, we are not built that way. We need to be built over. A new life needs to come in. And when the law has brought us to that point, and we cry out with Paul, "Wretched man that I am!" then the law has done its proper work. The tragic thing is that most Christians stop right there in their reading of the seventh chapter of Romans. They do not go on to the glorious word of deliverance. There is a way out. Paul has been in bondage under the law of sin. But a new law enters, and he exclaims, "The law of the Spirit ... made me free from the law of sin and of death." What is the new power of that law of the Spirit? *"Life in Christ Jesus."* What happens when the law of the Spirit is working, when we are enjoying the freedom indeed wherewith Christ hath set us free? *The requirement of the law is fulfilled in us.* This law of the Spirit, of the new Life in Christ Jesus, hath set us free from the law of sin and death, in order that we might keep the law of God. And it is kept in us just as long as we walk in the Spirit. God's plan is that we should walk in the Spirit all the time; that is "abiding in Christ." The struggle of the seventh of Romans is a struggle *under the law*, it is human effort apart from grace. It is not given as the normal Christian experience, but a parenthesis between two passages of glorious liberty, placed there to show what bearing the keeping of the law has upon the Christian's experience. The normal Christian experience is freedom from the dominion of sin.

What Grace Says

"Sin shall not have dominion over you: for ye are not under law but under grace." The secret of victory, therefore, is to keep under grace, which is walking in the Spirit. How is this to be done? All Christians who have real assurance of salvation see clearly that we are saved by grace. Law has condemned them. Law says "Do," and we cannot do.

Grace says, "Jesus Christ has done it for me."

"How much in the matter of my salvation has he done?"

"All of it."

"How much is there left for me to do?"

Nothing. "Faith does nothing"; faith believes that Jesus has done it all.

Now this is exactly the case with Christian living, and the keeping of the law of God. Whenever a Christian sins, sin is having dominion over him, and that means that he is living under law where he does not belong, and needs to get under grace. Here, just as in salvation from the penalty of sin, grace means that Jesus Christ is doing it all. What is left for me then in the matter of winning victory over sin? *Nothing.* Faith believes that Jesus is doing it all. That is grace, and nothing else is. For if my effort enters, it is not of grace, but partly by the work of the law. That is making void the grace of God, "for if righteousness is through the law, then Christ died for nought" (Gal. 2:21).

Christian liberty is changing the bondslavery of sin for the bondslavery of Christ; it is freedom from the law in order that the law may be kept in us by Another; it is changing the law that "made nothing perfect" for "the perfect law, the law of liberty." "So speak ye, and so do, as men that are to be judged by a law of liberty" (James 2:12).

GOD'S NEW SPELLING FOR "OBEY"

"TRUST and obey" is frequently given as the key to living the Victorious Life. "Surrender and obedience," another suggests as the things necessary for continuance in victory. Instant obedience to every word of God, another says, is absolutely necessary if one would be in victory. Another teacher points out that the New Testament reduces all God's commandments to two,—believe in Jesus and love one another,—and our duty is thus simplified: we are to obey these two commandments and victory is ours.

But to obey these commandments is exactly what I cannot do. If I obey these two commandments, the whole law of God is fulfilled in me. It is because I have failed to fulfil this perfect law of God, that I cry out with Paul, "Wretched man that I am! who shall deliver me?" The answer to that question gives me the secret of the Victorious Life, the Life that results in obedience. Of what avail is it to tell me that the secret of living the Victorious Life is to obey God, when the very reason I am hungry after the Life is because it *results* in obedience. That Life does what I have failed to do—obey God.

So long as we make obedience the cause or producer of victory, so long are we under the law. We are living under the Old Covenant. The law says, "He that doeth them [God's statutes] shall live in them"; that is, it is the law-keeper's obedience which brings life and victory.

But, it will be answered, when Christians are urged to obey it is not intended that they should do this in their own strength. We must constantly seek divine help to obey. There is the human side and the divine side. On our part we are to strive with all our willpower against sin, and God's part is to help us in the struggle.

Making Victory Impossible

There is one trouble with this program of human effort co-operating with divine power. *It always leads to defeat*, bringing the struggling man under the dominion of sin. It produces the man pictured in the seventh chapter of Romans. It is the program followed by nearly all Christians.

And that is why nearly all Christians are living in defeat practically all of the time.

It is not that defeats come now and again in the face of difficult temptations; the distressing thing in the experience of most earnest Christians is the consciousness that complete victory is *never* enjoyed; the occasional bad falls are but indications of a chronic condition of defeat.

The Two Covenants

The reason for this life of defeat is that Christians mingle law and grace, and this makes complete victory an impossibility. When we are in defeat it is because we are under the Old Covenant, which can make nothing perfect. It may be that we are clear intellectually on the distinction between law and grace, but it is the mingling of them in daily experience that results in defeat before sin. The secret of victory, then, is to get entirely from under law and get wholly under grace for the needs of the present moment. What does this mean? How can it be done?

Probably no one has put more concisely and clearly the distinction between the Old Covenant and the New than has Andrew Murray in his "Two Covenants." Under the Old Covenant, he points out, God says: "Obey me, and I will be your God." In the New Covenant God speaks in some such words as these: "I will put my law in your heart, and ye shall obey me." In the Old Covenant, Andrew Murray says, there were two parties, man and God. Man failed to keep his part of the agreement and the covenant was broken. In the New Covenant there is only one party. God undertakes the whole responsibility. The first is law. The second is grace. If man has any responsibility in the second, except to receive God's provision through faith, then it is no longer of free grace.

A clear-thinking Presbyterian elder, a man of culture and trained mind, who recently saw the truth of Christ as his victory for the first time, was asked what he thought was the difference between the Old Covenant of works and the New Covenant of Grace. Several verses of Scripture had just been quoted which brought out the distinction. He was a man of few words, and he answered by holding up two fingers of his left hand, and one finger of his right hand. He had seen at once, five minutes after entering into victory, what Andrew Murray makes the theme of his helpful book on the Spirit-filled life,—that in the New Covenant it is not man co-operating with God, but God assuming the whole work, and doing it for man.

"I Could Not Live Up to It"

Another Presbyterian elder, also a clear thinker, a lawyer of ability, was recently facing the question of the need of victory in his own life. When the Scripture promises were presented to him, and he was asked whether he would take victory, his reply was a decided "No."

"Why won't you?"

"Because I am not sure I could live up to it."

He still had two parties in his contract. He was still thinking under, and living under, the Old Covenant.

It sounds reasonable when a Christian says, "Of course, I am sure that *Christ* will always be faithful to his part, but the failure will come because of *my* weakness." When a Christian says that, he is not in victory; he has missed the very heart of the Victorious Life. He is still under the Old Covenant. For God made the New Covenant with full knowledge of that weakness of mine. Indeed *it was just because of that weakness of mine that the New Covenant was made.* Had the weakness not been there the Old Covenant would have sufficed. The New Covenant is of no avail, and means nothing, if it is not to operate in spite of that weakness.

Man's Part in Victory Over Sin

If God does everything in the matter of my obeying the law, what is my part? To do nothing. The human side of this New Covenant is to see that self is kept from doing anything, so that Grace may work. It is the effort of the self life, the human struggle described in Romans 7:7-24, which prevents the victory of Grace.

But surely Grace on God's part needs something on man's side if it is to be brought into touch with man. Yes, it needs to be told to man so that he may hear it as a message of good tidings. "Belief cometh of hearing, and hearing by the word of Christ" (Rom. 10:17). The word of good tidings to law-breaking Christians is that God has put his law in our hearts so that we shall obey him.

What are we to do with the word of good tidings? Believe it. If we do not believe that the law of the Spirit hath made us free from the law of sin, our unbelief does not affect the truth of God's word, but we ourselves lose the benefit of those good tidings. "For indeed we have had good tidings preached unto us, even as also they: but the word of hearing did not profit them, because it was not united by faith with them that heard" (Heb. 4:2).

"Obey" Becomes "Believe"

The "obey" of the Old Covenant has become in the New Covenant "believe." The responsibility for obedience has been taken entirely by Christ, and man's part is to believe that astounding fact. Christians are still urged to obey, but always the spelling of that word is "believe."

"Seeing ye have purified your souls in your obedience to the truth ... having been begotten again, not of corruptible seed, but of incorruptible, through the word of God.... But the word of the Lord abideth for ever. And this is the word of good tidings which was preached unto you.... For you therefore that believe is the preciousness: but for such as disbelieve, ... A stone of stumbling, and a rock of offence; for they stumble at the word, being disobedient."

These scattered verses in the first and second chapters of First Peter present the new spelling of the old "obey." Obedience to the truth is simply believing the word of good tidings, and they who stumbled at the word were disobedient because they did not believe the word of good tidings. It is a striking commentary that the King James Version uses "disobedient" in 1 Peter 2:7, where the Revised Version reads "disbelieve."

If this change from law to Grace is simply a different putting of the matter, leaving man's responsibility the same, then indeed there is no good tidings for the Christian in the matter of freedom from sin, and the Victorious Life teaching is a myth. If telling us to believe is just another way of asking us to obey, then are we no better off than before, and we must await our resurrection bodies in order to enjoy freedom from the law of sin against which we have been struggling. For with all our mind and heart we may want to obey, but there is that "different law in our members" preventing us from doing the things that we would. What is the new factor in Grace that changes everything? Is it something real, or something that I must produce by my own understanding, just a new *attitude* to the law?

Is Your Name in This Will?

It is something as real as the inheritance that a millionaire father wills to his son. God gives us a will in the third chapter of Galatians, and he speaks in it of an inheritance, and in words as carefully chosen and as accurate as in a perfect human will he explains who are the heirs in that will. The promise was given to Abraham and to his seed, not "seeds" as of many; "but as of one, and to thy seed, which is Christ" (Gal. 3:16). The closing verse of that will reveals the importance of that distinction the Holy Spirit makes between the singular and plural of the word seed. This distinction has puzzled scholars and some have called it an example of Paul's juggling with words, but it need not puzzle any of the heirs whose names are in this will. "And if ye are Christ's, then are ye Abraham's seed, heirs according to promise."

There is but one seed, Christ, and all that I am to get through this will, I get because I am in him. What is the inheritance promised in the will? If an earthly father knows how to will good gifts to his children, what shall be said of the heavenly Father's gift? The will says that it is "the promise of the Spirit" and that it is through faith (Gal. 3:14). The promise includes complete freedom from the law.

But does not the law also come from God? "Is the law then against the promises of God?" is a most natural question, and it is asked in this legal document which tells us of our inheritance. The answer to that question contains one of the most significant statements in the whole Word of God on the relation of law and grace: "God forbid: for if there had been a law given which could make alive, verily righteousness would have been of the law" (Gal. 3:21).

Where "High Ideals" Fall Down

There is as much difference, then, between being under law and under grace, as there is between a dead man and a live man. If a high ideal could have given life, the word tells us, if God could have provided a law which could make a dead man alive, Grace would not have been needed, for righteousness would have been by the law. The free gift of the New Covenant is a new LIFE. That is what the promise of the Spirit provides. Does this give a vivid light upon Romans 8:2, "The law of the Spirit ... made me free from the law of sin and of death?" And the power of the law of the Spirit is the resurrection life of Christ Jesus. So the complete verse reads, "The law of the Spirit of life in Christ Jesus made me free from the law of sin and of death."

The passage in Romans eight goes on to show how Jesus did for us the thing we could not do, and that as a result of what he did, and is doing through the Spirit, "the requirement of the law is fulfilled in us, who walk not after the flesh, but after the Spirit." If we are appropriating the promise of the Spirit, our inheritance through faith, *we are having fulfilled in us the law of God at this present moment.* That is what the Word of God says. That is what happens when we are under Grace and not under the law. Obedience to the law is guaranteed while we are under Grace,—walking in the Spirit. Disobedience to the law can come only when the Christian is living under law,—walking after the flesh.

But, some one asks, is not a Christian always under Grace? He is, in his *position*, and the Victorious Life is simply walking by faith in that position won by Christ. "We believed on Christ Jesus, that we might be justified by faith in Christ, and not by the works of the law: because by the works of the law shall no flesh be justified. But if, while we sought to be justified in Christ, we ourselves also were found sinners, is Christ a minister of sin? God forbid. For if I build up again those things which I destroyed, I prove myself a transgressor" (Gal. 2:16, 18).

A Christian Under Law

When a Christian sins, transgresses the law, he is building up that which he has destroyed.

He is acting as though he were back under the law.

He is doing the deeds of the old man that has been crucified with Christ.

He is denying the resurrection life of Christ which is in him.

He is walking after the flesh and not after the Spirit.

He is back on the basis of working instead of resting in the finished work of Christ.

He is under the works of the law instead of the hearing of faith.

He is not standing fast in the freedom wherewith Christ has set him free.

There is but one thing to be done in order to get back at once under grace and the faith life,—confess the sin and take cleansing in the blood of Jesus. This is wholly of Grace; no Christian would be so foolish as to try to atone for his sin or to help the Lord Jesus do a complete work of cleansing.

It is exactly the same sort of folly that leads the Christian to seek to add his own effort in the business of winning victory over the next temptation that assails him. "*If we live by the Spirit* [if we have been born again by the Spirit], *by the Spirit let us also walk*" (by the same supernatural power let us live day by day and hour by hour, letting God do it all by the Spirit) (Gal. 5:25).

God's new spelling for "obey" is "believe." And, as Mr. Trumbull put it to a Christian who was grieving because she did not have the faith to believe, "The faith for salvation is the faith for victory." Faith is just believing the word of God.

A Christian Under Grace

Have you believed the good tidings of future salvation and glory? Believe the same good tidings for present salvation from sin.

If you are under grace, sin shall not have dominion; you are walking in the Spirit.

Christ is dwelling in your heart by faith.

You are freed from the law with its works.

Yet the law of God is in your heart and it is your nature to keep it.

You are a new creation.

You are walking in newness of life.

You can finish the second chapter of Galatians as Paul finishes it: "For I through the law died unto the law, that I might live unto God. I have been crucified with Christ; and it is no longer I that live, but Christ liveth in me: and that life which I now live in the flesh I live in faith, the faith which is in the Son of God, who loved me, and gave himself up for me. I do not make void the grace of God" (Gal. 2:19-21).

WHEN TEMPTATION STRIKES

THERE is no state of grace that can be reached on earth which will guard a man from being tempted. The Victorious Life is a life of victory over temptation, but not a life of freedom from temptation.

Many a young Christian in the first flush of joy over new-found victory has somehow felt that this glorious new liberty was indeed freedom from temptation. For certain temptations have been taken completely out of the life. Perhaps it was the taste for tobacco, and the desire for smoking has been taken away. Or the questionable "border-line" amusements (questionable only to border-line Christians),—dancing and cards and the theater,—have completely lost their attractiveness and offer no temptation.

But suddenly, some day, temptation strikes from an unexpected quarter, and failure comes. It may be all over in a moment, but sin has entered. Perhaps it was a sudden flash of impatience, or irritation, or jealousy. Satan, close at hand, cunningly whispers, "You never had the experience of the Victorious Life.... And you never will." Or he whispers that still more cunning word, "This higher life business is all a mistake." And so the soul that has taken Christ as victory is often plunged into discouragement when the truth dawns that in the Victorious Life *temptations multiply*.

In this problem of temptation in the Victorious Life, as in every other conflict with our great Adversary, our safety must be found in the Word of God.

"Can a Dead Man Be Tempted?"

A common error regarding temptation in the Christian life is the belief that temptation is directed against a "sinful nature" within us. Some months ago there was discussed in Notes on Open Letters in *The Sunday School Times* the question of an earnest seeker who had taken Christ as his victory and was puzzled by this matter of temptation. He wrote:

How should temptation affect us? Christ had no sinful self in his temptation to contend with. Adam before the fall had not his sinful self to contend with; but we, since the fall, have a sinful self, even though we are in victory, if I understand rightfully. In Romans we read that the old man is crucified with him, that the body of sin might be destroyed, that henceforth we should not serve sin, for he that is dead is freed from sin. If we are dead why should evil thoughts or temptations of any kind find in us the slightest desire of yielding to them? What should be the effect of feeling them? A dead man has no life, has he?

Temptation is never aimed against a dead man, nor against evil in a man. There is no meaning in "tempting evil." There is no need for Satan to direct attacks against that which is already on his side. It is because we are alive and have power to sin that we are exhorted to reckon ourselves dead to—separated from—sin, not dead to temptation.

Temptation Hits Natural Desires

Temptation is directed against the *human* nature, and finds its entrance through the natural desires and impulses of the body. That is all Satan had to work upon in the case of Adam and Eve, and in the case of "the last Adam," our Lord himself. Both Adams were sinless men before temptation came,—and "the last Adam" was sinless after temptation came. But both lived in temptable bodies; and it is these human bodies, not any sin nature dwelling in us, that make temptation possible.

A lost man may have depraved and unnatural appetites, as the drink or drug habit, which drop off at regeneration. But the natural appetites remain, and through these temptation may come in many forms.

Satan has no other plan of temptation for Christians than that which he tried successfully upon the first Adam and with disastrous failure upon the last Adam. A study of these two conflicts with Satan reveals the startling fact that all our multiplied temptations come to us through three channels, and three only. If these citadels are held, victory is certain. To understand this not only simplifies the problem of temptation, but shows why certain *forms* of temptation fall away from the Christian who takes Christ as his victory, while *temptation* in many other forms remains.

Perhaps no one has summed up more concisely, in terms of everyday experience, these three channels of temptation, than does Professor Melvin Grove Kyle in his teaching on temptation in his seminary classes.

Our Three Desires

Dr. Kyle points out that man has three natural desires: (1) the desire to enjoy things; (2) the desire to get things; (3) the desire to do things.

These three cover the whole range of human desires. For the desire to *enjoy* things concerns everything that has to do with a man's body. The desire to *get* things concerns everything that a man sees outside of himself, the things that he can obtain in one way or another for himself. The desire to *accomplish* things includes everything that goes out from the man to affect in one way or another that outside world. Professor Kyle's suggested definition of temptation is this: "Temptation is the incitement of a natural desire to go beyond the bound set by God."

With this analysis before us, let us look into what happened when Satan came to our first parents. Let it be remembered that none of these three desires necessarily has to do with sin. Adam and Eve had these desires before sin entered. Our Lord Jesus had these same natural human desires.

Sin is doing something that God has told man not to do, or not doing something that God has told him to do. Eve's failure began, under temptation, when she was willing to consider Satan's questioning of God's word.

Eve's Threefold Temptation

"And when the woman saw that the tree was good for food, and that it was a delight to the eyes, and that the tree was to be desired to make one wise, she took of the fruit thereof, and did eat." There was the threefold temptation. "She saw that the tree was good for food"; her desire to enjoy things was incited, and she faced the question of satisfying in an unlawful way that desire for enjoyment. She saw that the fruit was "a delight to the eyes": her desire to get the attractive thing she saw was incited, and she faced the question of whether she should satisfy that desire in a way that God had forbidden. Finally she saw that the tree was "to be desired to make one wise." Satan had told her that she and her husband would be as God if they ate the fruit. Her desire to accomplish things took the form of reaching out after equality with God.

Now turn for a moment to the analysis of sin and temptation that the Holy Spirit gives in 1 John 2:16: "For all that is in the world, the lust of the flesh, and the lust of the eyes, and the vainglory of life, is not of the Father, but is of the world." Here is an inclusive statement of all that is in the world. The apostle is stating here the only three ways in which it is possible for a man to sin. Note that they are the three points at which Eve failed.

When the desire to *enjoy things* goes beyond the bounds set by God it becomes "the lust of the flesh." The lawful desire to *get things*, when it turns into sin, becomes "the lust of the eyes." When the desire *to do things* leads a man away from God, it becomes "the vainglory [or the pride] of life."

Dr. Kyle points out in his study of temptation that Eve fell at *every* point of her nature, and sinned in "the lust of the flesh, the lust of the eyes, and the vainglory of life." He notes also that the lust of the eyes and the pride of life had no immediate outlet of expression for Adam and Eve, situated as they were in the midst of a world that was all theirs, and so the sin found immediate expression in some form of the lust of the flesh. Yet man had yielded and sinned at all three points.

Tempting Our Sinless Lord

Turning now from the luxurious garden to the barren wilderness, the same Tempter comes to our Lord Jesus, the last Adam, when he was hungry after his fasting of forty days and forty nights; and the Tempter came with the same three appeals. Our Lord Jesus had the natural desire to enjoy food for his body. He was hungry, and the desire was right. But the Tempter asked him to satisfy that hunger in a wrong way. Satan again begins his attack by a question. He does not hold before Christ the temptation to *become* as God. He raises the question as to whether he is the Son of God, and suggests that this be proved by making use of the omnipotence of the Creator to satisfy his own human needs. It was far more subtle than the appeal to Eve's desire to enjoy the fruit; but at the bottom it was an attack on the Word of God. Our Lord's answer not only checkmates the Tempter, but states a profound truth by which his brethren may enter into victory under similar temptations. "Man shall not live by bread alone, but by every word that proceedeth out of the mouth of God."

Our Lord had a natural desire to get things. What he desired to get was "all the kingdoms of the world." They belonged to him. He came to earth to secure them. Satan strikes at this perfectly right desire to get things by showing our Lord all the kingdoms of the world, and the glory of them, "and he said unto him, All these things will I give thee if thou wilt fall down and worship me." The desire to get these kingdoms was right; but the temptation was to get them in some way not of God's ordering. Making a step outside the will of God always means exchanging the worship of God for the worship of Satan; and so our Lord answers: "Get thee hence, Satan; for it is written, Thou shalt worship the Lord thy God, and him only shalt thou serve."

Our Lord also had that third desire, the desire to accomplish things. The work he came to accomplish was to bring redemption—to the Jew first, and also to the Gentile. He came to his own with the desire that they should recognize him as the One sent from God, their Messiah. Satan strikes at this right desire, and presents to Jesus a quick way to accomplish this purpose. But again it is a way with a question mark regarding God's Word.

It has been suggested that the thought here is that Jesus could prove to the multitude gathered below in the temple court that he was indeed the Son of God when this Messianic prophecy was fulfilled before their eyes in such a startling way. The reply of our Lord is significant. "Again it is written, Thou shalt not make trial of the Lord thy God." This quotation from Deuteronomy 6:16 refers back to the incident at Rephidim when the children of Israel made trial of Jehovah by saying: "Is Jehovah among us, or not?" (Exod. 17:7.) So Satan asked Jesus to prove that God's Word was indeed true, and settle the fact that he was the Son of God and that Jehovah was indeed with him.

As our first parents fell at all three points of attack, so our Lord won the victory at every point. Borrowing again an illuminating suggestion from Dr. Kyle's study of the subject, we have here the real explanation of that word concerning our Lord that he was tempted in all points like as we are. He was tempted on every side of his nature. He did not necessarily meet every individual form of temptation that has come to other men, but he did meet the Adversary at these three points, which comprise all the possible area of temptation.

The victory over temptation has been won. His victory is a guarantee of our triumph over every form of temptation that can ever meet us. It is ours to choose whether we shall share in that victory already won by our Elder Brother, or be united with the first Adam in his defeat.

THE CONQUEST OF TEMPTATION

THE Word of God never offers freedom from temptation. But it does offer to Christians victory over all temptation. One of Satan's lies that has been accepted as almost an axiom in the thinking and the experience of Christians is that no one can expect victory over every one of his temptations. But God says: "There hath *no* temptation taken you but such as man can bear: But God is faithful, who will not suffer you to be tempted above that ye are able; but will with the temptation make also the way of escape, that ye may be able to endure it" (1 Cor. 10:13). It is significant that this verse is immediately preceded by a word of warning: "Wherefore let him that thinketh he standeth take heed lest he fall."

There is ever before the Christian the possibility of falling. There is no state of grace from which he may not, before some temptation, step into awful sin. But God's Word, which cannot be broken, stands pledged to us that in *every* temptation there is "the way of escape." And our Lord Jesus is "the Way." Victory over temptation was won by Christ. Satan is an already defeated foe. Defeat in temptation came to Adam. It is for every man, and every Christian, to decide whether he will share the first Adam's defeat or the last Adam's victory.

The two great temptation scenes pictured in the Bible, that of our first parents and that of our Lord, show that temptation finds its way into the human heart through three avenues. When man falls before these temptations the resulting sins are what the Apostle describes as "the lust of the flesh and the lust of the eyes and the vainglory of life." Let us see how this Bible picture of the sins that are in the world corresponds with conditions in the twentieth century.

Africa's Three Sins

A missionary recently back from the heart of Africa was describing some of the intimate things that she had learned regarding the natives. As she spoke of the daily life of the natives, and told of the chief problems of missionary work, there were three outstanding sins that were emphasized. There is the gross immorality, which came up for mention in connection with the description of the tribal dances and what they lead to. There is the grasping after possessions, a tendency to covetousness that is so deeply imbedded in their natures that the missionaries need to exercise the greatest care in dealing with new converts. This native quality came vividly to the missionary's mind when she was speaking of the native Christian evangelists and the problem of compensating them in such a way that the old cupidity will not be aroused. A third characteristic of the native in all the villages is his consuming desire to secure a high place in the "Four Hundred" of his tribe. There are distinct social honors, and for many of the young men the passion of life is to win these honors.

This missionary had no intention of analyzing the outstanding sins of the natives, but these three things naturally came before her as she described their daily life. And these three comprise "all that is in the world, the lust of the flesh and the lust of the eyes and the vainglory of life."

Put into briefer form these three sins are lust, covetousness, pride. All sin comes under one or other of these three classes.

America's Three Sins

These three are the outstanding sins of America. Dan Crawford came out of Africa into civilization just about the time the "newer" forms of dancing were having their first popularity. He made the startling statement that he had seen all of these unspeakably vile dances in pagan Africa. In America, he said, they were only in a new setting. Essentially they were the same, and *they were for the same purpose*. What we call the gross sin of the African flourishes in every civilized land.

Those who read a business man's article, published several years ago in *The Sunday School Times*, on "The Sin That We Are Afraid to Mention," will not soon forget his arraignment of the awful sin of covetousness, "which is idolatry." And it was *in the Christian church* that this layman found the black sin that Christians keep quiet about. What then shall be said of covetousness in the business world?

There is finally that climax of all sins of America, and of man, the sin of pride, most subtle and most pervading of all, the sin that will culminate in man's final defiance of God. Saddest of all, it is this sin which appears at its ugliest when it takes the form of spiritual pride in the life of one who is zealous to serve God and to be wholly yielded to him.

In a message that S. D. Gordon gave on temptation he remarked that there are three chief avenues by which Satan reaches men. He stated the three in these brief words: "Sex," "Money," "I." It is exactly the classification that God makes in his Word. If, by his grace, we get victory at these three points, then indeed are we free from the dominion of sin.

So much for the *sin* that results when man falls before one or another of these temptations. But what of the temptations themselves? How do they affect a Christian who is trusting Christ for victory? What is the practical bearing on the common temptations that meet us in everyday life? Then there is the final, most important question, what is the way to prevent these desires from conceiving and bringing forth sin?

Why Not Freedom from Temptation?

A *Sunday School Times* reader has written of his experience. "It is not a temptation for me to take a glass of beer; there is nothing in me that requires or desires it; but sometimes it might be and has been a strong temptation to get impatient, which I have yielded to at times. Why should one be any more a temptation than the other, provided I am in victory over all sin?"

Careful distinction must be made between temptation itself and the form that the temptation may take. The appeal to a man's natural desires may change its form, but always, in every part of his nature, he will be tempted while he is in this mortal body. The desire for beer which leads to intemperance and sin is an appeal to a natural appetite. Sin is moral, and does not reside in the physical appetites, which are merely the channels for the temptation and sin. A man who has been in bondage to drink may through the power of Christ completely lose that desire and have no further temptation to that particular form of appetite. But the temptation to intemperance remains. For the natural appetites remain. While the appetite may give up this taste or that, and thus be dead to certain *forms* of temptation, the Christian is always liable to the temptation to go contrary to the will of God, in satisfying these natural appetites of the body: hunger, the sacred sex desire, and all the natural impulses of the body that may seek expression in lawful ways.

The *Times* reader compares his freedom from the temptation to drink with the appeal that is made to him to get impatient. But strictly speaking, one is never tempted to be impatient. No one desires to be impatient, and Satan could not use any incentive to such a temptation. Yet we sometimes speak of these temptations to irritability, jealousy, loss of temper, as though there were some secret springs in our nature labeled "Impatience," "Irritability," and like qualities, and that the temptation consisted in Satan touching these springs and causing the sin. A business man does not lose his temper for the sake of the pleasure it gives him. It may be an intense desire to have justice that has led to his outbreak against some one who has dealt unfairly. The temptation has come along the line of some natural desire. So with the housekeeper who is irritated with her maid over some bit of stupidity, or the young girl who is "blue" and moody because her plans for the day's enjoyment have been upset.

Temptation Remains—Its Form Changes

Thus it is that while a Christian who yields utterly to God and accepts Christ as his victory may instantly be free from even the temptation to drink, or to smoke, or to indulge in worldly amusements, or to do a hundred and one things that he has been accustomed to do, the temptations to the root-sins of lust and covetousness and pride *will remain with him*. They will take more subtle forms. Satan cannot tempt him now in the grosser, worldly way. He will now take advantage of this one's very zeal for God, and will make appeal to his earnest devotion to God's service to lead into sins of impatience and irritation and jealousy and pride.

In the face of these temptations, what is the guarantee against failure which the victorious Christian has, and which the man of the world knows nothing of? When a Christian wholly yields his life to the mastery of the Lord Jesus he has still the desire to enjoy things, the desire to get things, and the desire to accomplish things. Christ does not kill the natural desires. *It is the old self-life that Christ wants to put to death.* That is why a Christian must share in present experience the crucifixion-death of his Lord before he can share his victory over temptation. This is what surrender of self means for the Christian who desires victory. He must, moment by moment, reckon himself to be dead unto sin. He is not dead to temptation, for his natural human desires are still there.

Desires Remain—Their Object Changes

In the Christian who has learned the full secret of victory these natural desires are lifted to a new plane. His desires now do not center in the old self-life. They center in Christ. To him to live is Christ. His whole desire is Christ. He still desires to enjoy things, but only in a way that shall glorify God. He desires to get things, but to get them for God, not for self. His desire to accomplish things is to do things for God.

This does not mean that the victorious Christian will not be open to fierce temptations, just as our Lord was,—real temptations that require a real conquest. But as he abides in Christ, accepting by faith the victory that Christ already has won, instead of striving to struggle against these assaults of the enemy, the temptations remain merely *temptations*, and do not pass into the *sins* of lust or covetousness or pride.

These three channels of temptation appear to correspond in a remarkable way with the three-fold nature of man—body, soul and spirit. And for the man in victory all these are Christ's. Here is the human body with all the natural appetites intact. But the Christian who is reckoning the old self-life to be dead knows that this body now, with all its natural desires, is "for the Lord; and the Lord for the body" (1 Cor. 6:13), for "Know ye not that your body is a temple of the Holy Spirit that is in you, that ye have from God? and ye are not your own; for ye were bought with a price: glorify God therefore in your body" (1 Cor. 6:19, 20).

The Secret of the Single Eye

There are in the victorious Christian not only the desires of the body but the desires of the soul. For may we not say that the sin of "the lust of the eye" is a sin of the "soulish" part of a man's nature? It concerns his desire to acquire the things that he sees. To the natural man these things are riches to be obtained for himself. "He that hath an evil eye hasteth after riches" (Proverbs 28:22). The wise man here connects covetousness and "the evil eye." Let us hear the words of the Master of wise men: "Lay not up for yourselves treasures upon the earth, where moth and rust doth consume and where thieves break through and steal: but lay up for yourselves treasures in heaven, where neither moth nor rust doth consume, and where thieves do not break through nor steal: for where thy treasure is, there will thy heart be also. The lamp of the body is the eye: if therefore thine eye be single, thy whole body shall be full of light. But if thine eye be evil, thy whole body shall be full of darkness. If therefore the light that is in thee be darkness, how great is the darkness! No man can serve two masters: for either he will hate the one, and love the other; or else he will hold to the one, and despise the other. Ye cannot serve God and mammon" (Matthew 6:19-24).

Here is the clear choice. The desire to get the riches we see may become the lust of the eye, covetousness, the servant of mammon. But the Christian abiding in Christ has a "single eye," that is, he has but one passion, to lay up treasure in heaven. He has not a doubtful mind as to whether he may grasp after this or that. He has but a single question, as his eye is single, and that is how may he glorify God in his getting? He makes use indeed of the mammon of unrighteousness, but not for self's sake,—for the sake of Another.

The Most Subtle Sin

May we not call the most subtle sin of all, the sin of pride, a sin of the spirit? The victorious Christian still has the desire to accomplish things. Indeed this desire is intensified a thousandfold. To the natural man this desire centers wholly in self, whether he knows it or not. But one in whom the old self-life is dead cries with Paul, "God forbid that I should glory save in the cross of our Lord Jesus Christ, by whom the world is crucified unto me, and I unto the world" (Gal. 6:14). With the psalmist he sings: "My soul shall make her boast in Jehovah: The meek shall hear thereof, and be glad. O, magnify Jehovah with me, and let us exalt His name together" (Psalm 34:2, 3). "In God have we made our boast all the day long, and we will give thanks unto thy name forever" (Psalm 44:8). This sort of boasting leads not to self pride but to meekness. "Thus saith Jehovah, Let not the wise man glory in his wisdom, neither let the mighty man glory in his might. Let not the rich man glory in his riches: but let him that glorieth glory in this, that he understandeth, and knoweth me, that I am Jehovah, who exercise lovingkindness, justice, and righteousness, in the earth" (Jeremiah 9:23).

All desires of life, then, for the Christian who abides in victory, center in Christ. "And whatsoever ye do, in word or in deed, do all in the name of the Lord Jesus, giving thanks to God the Father through him" (Col. 3:17).

And conquest of temptation is not a negative matter. Love is the fulfilling of the law, and only the heart filled with that love which is Christ can know freedom from lust, covetousness, and pride. Back of these three outward sins, there is the inward nature which has departed from God. Perhaps no one in our day has pointed out more clearly the three great sins of omission than has Miss Louisa Vaughan, of China. She calls these the "Christian sins": Failure to love the Lord our God with all our heart and strength and mind; failure to love one another as Christ loved us; failure to believe on Christ so that the works that he did and greater works than these should be wrought through us. These Christian sins, Miss Vaughan insists, must be confessed and cleansed in the blood of Jesus before the fulness of the Spirit can be enjoyed. To have these commandments fulfilled in us is the Victorious Life. And only when this root-condition of unlove and unbelief (which are really one, for "love believeth all things") is dealt with shall we know freedom from lust and covetousness and pride.

HOW JESUS LIVED THE VICTORIOUS LIFE

IN WHAT sense was Jesus a man as we are? We read that he was tempted in all points like as we are, yet without sin. But have you ever asked, Of what comfort or strength is it to me that he was tempted in all points as I am, *if he was without sin?* It is just because *I am not without sin* that I fall before these temptations.

Is it true after all that the Lord Jesus was a man as I am?

Was not the real secret of his victory over sin the fact that he was God?

Is not the secret of my defeat the fact that I am just a man and not God?

The answer to these questions reveals one of the richest secrets in the Word concerning the real meaning of the Victorious Life. For we shall find this startling truth, that if we are to live the Victorious Life at all we must live it by the same rule as Jesus of Nazareth lived it.

Christ had to come to earth to show us what man is like. A needed emphasis has been put upon the truth that our Lord came to earth to reveal the Father,—to show men what God is like. But it was just as necessary that our Lord should reveal what God intended *man* to be.

If we wish to know what God is like there is but one thing to do: look at Jesus. So there is no way of discovering what a true man is like except by looking at Jesus. He is the only "man," in the true sense of the word, who has lived since sin entered the human race. Through the fall man lost the image of God, and from that day until our Lord came there was no example of man as God intended him to be.

A mistaken notion, encouraged by the poets, prevails quite commonly, that to sin is human; to forgive, divine. Whatever the measure of truth in the little sentiment, the error in it is more dangerous. To sin is not human; it is devilish. Sin is no part of man as God planned him to be. And so our Lord represents in himself what God intended a man to be, and he lived according to that plan.

The One True "Man"

The name for himself most often upon the lips of our Master was "the Son of man." A notable Greek scholar has recently pointed out that this expression means far more than a son of a human parent. It rather suggests that gathered up into this Son of man are all the qualities of what "man" is. So, may we not say that as the fulness of God dwelt in him bodily so did the fulness of man dwell in him?

Some one has suggested that God did wonderful things through the Lord Jesus not because Jesus was God, but because he was perfect man. What does this really mean in terms of our everyday life?

Nowhere in Scripture is there such a remarkable setting forth, first of the deity of our Lord, then of his humanity, side by side, as in the first and second chapters of the Epistle to the Hebrews. "God, having of old time spoken unto the fathers in the prophets by divers portions and in divers manners, hath at the end of these days spoken unto us in a Son."

"Very God of Very God"

Thus the wonderful epistle opens; and then that Son is presented first as one who expresses the very image of the substance of God. He is compared with angels, and shown to be infinitely above them. God the Father speaks of his angels as messengers; he addresses the Son: "thy throne, O *God*." In the second chapter again are angels compared, this time with man. The same Son is shown to be made for a little while lower than the angels, taking the form of man.

In this first chapter of Hebrews the Holy Spirit, when he seeks to attest the truth that Jesus is God, calls the Old Testament to witness, and two groups of three quotations each are made, each time the words being put in the mouth of God the Father. In the second chapter when the Spirit seeks to press home the parallel truth that Jesus is a man, one with us, he uses a group of three quotations from the Old Testament. In these quotations we shall discover something of the preciousness for us of the truth that the Lord Jesus was a man, one with his brethren. "For both he that sanctifieth and they that are sanctified are all of one: for which cause he is not ashamed to call them brethren, saying ..." (Heb. 2:11).

Then there follow in the twelfth and thirteenth verses of the second chapter of Hebrews the three quotations from the Old Testament.

This is the first:

"I will declare thy name unto my brethren,

In the midst of the congregation will I sing thy praise."

One With Our Lord in Resurrection

This is the twenty-second verse of the twenty-second Psalm, the Crucifixion Psalm. But the twenty-second Psalm is more than a crucifixion Psalm; it is a resurrection Psalm as well. This twenty-second verse that the Spirit uses to prove that Jesus is one with us is the first verse of the resurrection half of the Psalm. When our Lord rose from the dead he said, "Go unto my brethren, and say to them, I ascend unto my Father and your Father, and my

God and your God" (John 20:17). This was the first time that our Lord linked those words "my Father and your Father." For in his resurrection he was in a new way "the firstborn of many brethren." "Thou art my Son, this day have I begotten thee," was not spoken of the eternal generation of the Son of God, the living Word who was not begotten on a day but was before all time. Neither do the words refer to the glad day when the babe was born of the Virgin. They refer to that glad resurrection day when in a new way he declared God's name unto his brethren. This is made clear in Acts 13:32, 33: "And we bring you good tidings of the promise made unto the fathers, that God hath fulfilled the same unto our children, in that he raised up Jesus; as also it is written in the second psalm, Thou art my Son, this day have I begotten thee."

We are one with our elder Brother, then, in death and resurrection, and here is the death-blow to Satan's lie of universal brotherhood and universal fatherhood. The firstborn of many brethren is brother only to those who share in his death that they may share also in his new birth.

One With Our Lord as Witnesses

The third word from the Old Testament quoted in the second chapter of Hebrews which attests the humanity of our Lord is this: "Behold, I and the children whom God hath given me." These words from Isaiah 8:18 were originally from the lips of Isaiah, who said: "Behold, I and the children whom God hath given are for signs and for wonders in Israel for Jehovah of hosts." Dr. W. J. Erdman once remarked that when Isaiah's two sons walked along the streets of Jerusalem they were living sermons for the children of Israel to read. The name of one was "Mahershalal-hash-baz," and whenever an Israelite looked upon this son he heard God saying to him "the spoil speedeth, the prey hasteth." If he believed God he knew that this was a prophecy of the terrific judgment of God that was to fall on a sinning nation. Isaiah's other son was "Shear-jashub," or "the remnant shall return," and the discerning Israelite who could read this sermon aright saw in it the glad hope of God's grace in the day of judgment saving a remnant of those who put their trust in him. The name of the father of these two sons, "Isaiah," means "the salvation of Jehovah."

Evidently the thought is that our Lord and we, his brethren, are still for signs and wonders in setting forth the salvation of Jehovah in its two phases, of terrific judgment that is to come upon a disobedient world and the glad message of salvation to the remnant who shall believe.

The second quotation from the Old Testament used in the second chapter of Hebrews to prove our Lord's true humanity is in these remarkable words: "I will put my trust in him." How can this quotation have any bearing on the fact that he is our brother and that he lived down here as a man?

The Heart-Throbs of Our Human Lord

The quotation is from the second verse of Psalm eighteen: "The Lord is my rock, and my fortress, and my deliverer; my God, my strength, in whom I will trust." These originally are "the words of David, the servant of the Lord, who spake unto the Lord the words of this song in the day that the Lord delivered him from the hand of all his enemies, and from the hand of Saul." But, as a noted Bible teacher has pointed out, the Holy Spirit put into the mouth of David words that went infinitely beyond his own experience, words that could only be fulfilled in their true meaning when the greater Son of David came and met the forces of evil that were faintly foreshadowed by the enemies David met.

Read through the eighteenth Psalm as the words of the Lord Jesus. It is an inspired description of the awful conflict of the powers of darkness against the Son of man, when he tasted death for every man. Have you ever wondered why there were not given to us in the four Gospels more intimate glimpses of the human heart-throbs of Jesus? Have you wished that you might enter somewhat into the meaning of Gethsemane, rather than to have him go into the garden alone? Read in the eighteenth and other Messianic Psalms the human heart-throbs of the Son of man.

"I love thee, O Jehovah, my strength.

Jehovah is my rock, and my fortress, and my deliverer;

My God, my rock, in whom I will take refuge;

My shield, and the horn of my salvation, my high tower.

I will call upon Jehovah, who is worthy to be praised;

So shall I be saved from mine enemies.

The cords of death compassed me,

And the floods of ungodliness made me afraid.

The cords of Sheol were round about me;

The snares of death came upon me."

HIS Secret of Victory

Read on in the Psalm the description of this conflict with the supernatural powers of evil, and find in it the secret of our Lord's victory over them. *He did not count upon any strength in himself. He looked to another.* He was a man, and if there was to be any strength in him for victory over that supernatural enemy, that strength must come from another. The secret of our Lord's victory was just this: "I will put my trust in him."

The Holy Spirit made no mistake in his selection of Old Testament passages when he wished to show that it behooved this Saviour of ours "in all things to be made like unto his brethren," and that "in that he himself hath suffered being tempted, he is able to succor them that are tempted" (Heb. 2:17, 18).

Jesus lived the Victorious Life, not because he was God, but because he was perfect man; he lived as God planned that man should live. In a very true sense (though the statement would need certain qualification), our Lord took to himself no more advantage in the matter of winning victory over temptations than have we, his brethren.

Why He Emptied Himself

But *he* was *God*. Yes, all the fulness of the Godhead was in him, or he could not have made atonement for the sins of his brethren. But remember that Christ Jesus emptied himself. This does not mean that he ceased in any sense to be God. But there was something that he had as God, in glory with the Father, that he did not have as the God-man living here on earth. He was rich up there; he was poor down here (2 Cor. 8:9). Of what did Jesus empty himself? He emptied himself of the glory that he had with the Father before the world was. The full meaning of that none of us can fathom. But here again there is a very practical application to our everyday living of this profound doctrine of the humiliation of our Lord:

He emptied himself of that which would have prevented him, in the days of his suffering on earth, from being a true Son of man.

Jesus voluntarily gave up that inherent power that was his as God, and lived his life as God intended that man should live his life, *in utter dependence on a power not his own.*

When man fell, his sin was a declaration of independence of God. He thus made impossible the living of a true man's life, for an essential part of a man's life is to live moment by moment in utter dependence on another, his Maker.

That is why our Lord constantly pointed *away from himself.* "The Son can do nothing of himself" (John 5:19). "I can of myself do nothing: as I hear, I judge: and my judgment is righteous; because I seek not mine own will, but the will of him that sent me" (John 5:30). "I do nothing of myself, but as the Father taught me, I speak these things" (John 8:28). "The words that I say unto you I speak not from myself: but the Father abiding in me doeth his works" (John 14:10). Our Lord here speaks as the Son of man, not coming in his own name, or living in his own name, but in the name and by the power of Another dwelling within him.

The Son of Man's Watchword

The secret of the Son of man, plainly written across the record of his earthly conflicts, is surrender and faith. "Not I, but the Father." And "as the Father hath sent me, even so send I you" (John 20:21).

The Son of man's watchword is, "I will put my trust in him." Only man can say that. Glorified God cannot say that.

Whenever man says, "I will put my trust in Him," and means it, all the omnipotence of the risen and indwelling Lord of resurrection life is available for him, and victory is certain.

SERVING WITH "THE MIND OF CHRIST"

"TRULY he was the servant of all," said a friend of J. Hudson Taylor's as he concluded a narration of some incidents in the life of the great missionary in China. Hudson Taylor was like his Master. Only in so far as the service of any of us Christians is after the example of our Lord is it real service.

In the study of "How Jesus Lived the Victorious Life," it was seen that Christ emptied himself in order that he might live as a man and open the way for his brethren to win the victory *in the same way that he won it.* Jesus lived down here as God intended a man should live—in utter, moment by moment, dependence upon Another, and in the last study it was pointed out that our Victory motto must be the motto that Jesus lived by: "I will put my trust in *Him*." It is our purpose now to view this truth in particular relation to the service of a Christian, and to examine more closely the meaning of Christ's "emptying" that we may know wherein he was our example in service.

It is not primarily the acts in the life of Jesus that furnish us our example in service. Many of the recorded activities of Christ, the things he did and the things he said, are by their very nature,—their uniqueness,—deeds and words that we cannot imitate. It is the mind of Christ we are to have. Then shall we have the secret of the spirit and the power of his service.

The great passage in the second chapter of Philippians on the humiliation of our Lord deals with profound mysteries of the eternal world, yet it touches in the most vital way the everyday life and service of the Christian. It concerns the sending of Christ Jesus out of Glory with the Father into the world of men and sin. How startling, then, that our Lord should take such a sublime event, which goes too deep for utterance, and bring it to our very doorsteps, when he says: "As the Father hath sent me into the world even so send I you into the world."

"Have this mind in you which was also in Christ Jesus," the Apostle enjoins. What is "this mind"? How are we to have it? Paul goes on to describe it: "Who, existing in the form of God, counted not the being on an equality with God a thing to be grasped, but emptied himself, taking the form of a servant, being made in the likeness of men; and being found in fashion as a man, he humbled himself, becoming obedient unto death, yea, the death of the cross" (Phil. 2:5-8).

The Mind of Satan

Something of the significance of this sublime passage and the verses that immediately follow, will be seen if we place beside it another picture which also concerns the mysteries of the eternal world and the throne of God. It is found in the fourteenth chapter of Isaiah: "How art thou fallen from heaven,

O day star, son of the morning! how art thou cut down to the ground, that didst lay low the nations! And thou saidst in thy heart, I WILL ascend into heaven, I WILL exalt my throne above the stars of God; and I WILL sit upon the mount of congregation, in the uttermost parts of the north: I WILL ascend above the heights of the clouds; I WILL make myself like the Most High" (Isa. 14:12-14).

This is a portion of "a parable against the king of Babylon." In it we have undoubtedly the picture of the great Adversary of the Lord Jesus Christ, Satan, the highest of created beings; here is a glimpse of his fall and the secret of it. So striking is the contrast that it is hard to escape the conviction that the Spirit intended this to be related to the passage in Philippians that tells of our Lord's emptying. This contrast is one that runs from beginning to end through the Scriptures, which are, indeed, the record of the conflict between these two beings, the Son of God who became also the Son of man, and the "son of the morning," who became the son of uttermost darkness.

Pride Incarnate and Humility Incarnate.

The Son of God was the Word, who was in the beginning with God, and was God. But though he possessed that equality he did not esteem it a thing to be grasped after, but he emptied himself of the glory that was his own. The other glorious being, exalted though he was among the hosts of God, was not in the form of God; he was but a creature of the Most High. But he essayed to grasp the equality that was not his: "I will make myself like the Most High." Mark now the terrific climax in each of these descriptions. The Son of God in becoming the Son of man took step after step in his humiliation, lower and lower, until he touched the bottom in the cursed death of the cross: "becoming obedient unto death, yea, the death of the cross." Then immediately follows this word: "Wherefore also God highly exalted him, and gave unto him the name which is above every name; that in the name of Jesus every knee should bow, of things in heaven and things on earth and things under the earth, and that every tongue should confess that Jesus is Lord, to the glory of God the Father." Satan sought to climb higher and higher until his ambition reached after the Godhead: "I will make myself like the Most High." Immediately follows this word: "Thou shalt be brought down to hell, to the uttermost parts of the pit."

There is more in the passages, however, than these two tremendous contrasts of humiliation and attempted exaltation, and then of exaltation and uttermost destruction. Jesus told his followers that he was sending them into the world as the Father sent him. His great Adversary likewise sends men into the world to carry out the spirit of his ambition. So he came to our first parents in the garden, and the temptation was that they should imitate him in seeking to be like God. They fell before the temptation and the sin was, essentially, a declaration of independence of God. From that day on every sin, whether the sin of an unbeliever or the sin of a born-again Christian, has resulted because of this independence of God. The conflict of that eternal world has thus been projected into the world of men. The Son of God and the Prince of demons are contending for this world, and the principles underlying the conflict are clearly set forth in these passages that have been before us.

Satan's Coming Man

This conflict is to have a climax. The sin of man will head up in the Man of Sin. This is he who shall come in the spirit and power of Satan, the false Messiah. Jesus forewarned of his coming, when he said: "I am come in my Father's name, and ye receive me not: if another shall come in his own name, him ye will receive" (John 5:43). The Isaiah passage describes not only the scene in heaven when Satan reached after the throne of God, but it foreshadows the Man of Sin on earth, "the son of perdition, he that opposeth and exalteth himself against all that is called God or that is worshiped; so that he sitteth in the temple of God, setting himself forth as God ... even he, whose coming is according to the working of Satan with all power and signs and lying wonders, and with all deceit of unrighteousness for them that perish; because they received not the love of the truth, that they might be saved. And for this cause God sendeth them a working of error, that they should believe a lie" (2 Thess. 2:3, 4, 9-11).

Man's Final Religion

The spirit of Satan, then, finds its climax in the worship of man, rather than the worship of God. Here is the heart of all sin. This is the central lie of Satan by which he deceives men. The final religion of man, before the coming of the Lord Jesus to earth again, will be the religion of humanity, the worship of man as the only deity. Paul brings all men who reject God's revelation under this condemnation: "They exchanged the truth of God for a lie, and worshipped and served the creature rather than the Creator, who is blessed for ever."

We have been speaking of the great conflict of the ages between Jesus and his Adversary, the conflict that underlies the raging of the nations to-day, as Satan works out his plan to put the creature in the place of the Creator, to send that one, inspired of Satan, who will come in his own name and who will be received because he comes as man. But this same conflict goes on in each individual life.

Every man, because God has given him free will, must make his choice as to which of these he will follow, the Son of man, or the Man of Sin. Even the Christian, who has made his choice, will find constantly before him the possibility of serving in the spirit of his Lord or in the spirit of Satan.

When the Christian is not serving after the example of the Lord Jesus, let him ponder this well,—that he is serving after the spirit of Satan. How startled must Peter have been when the Lord not only told him he savored of the things of men (the spirit of Satan), but actually addressed him as Satan, knowing that it was the great Adversary he was meeting again in one of his loved disciples. Very often is it true of Christians that "ye know not what spirit ye are of." Is it too much to say that much of the service that is being offered to-day in the name of Christ, by followers of His, is mixed with the spirit of the evil one?

Testing Our Service

What is that spirit of the evil one? It is written large in the two words that stand out in that Isaiah passage: "I WILL." Set these words against those other words: "Not my will, but thine." Now let us set these words against our own Christian service and answer the question as to whether it is after the example of the Son of man. What is it to have the mind of Christ?

In three respects is there danger that our Christian service shall lack the mind of Christ. We may work zealously *in the energy of the flesh*. The old self-life is not reckoned dead, crucified with Christ. If we have the mind of Christ we must become conformed to his death, even as he was obedient unto the death of the cross. There are thousands of Christians who are doing good things but doing them in the energy of the flesh, without the Spirit of God. If we would have the mind of Christ we must have that old self-life crucified, for Christian service done in the flesh cannot please God.

Consecrated Christians who have really surrendered the old self-life may work zealously *in the energy of the soul*. There is the danger of forcing results that look good but are really not the product of the Spirit of God. Service after the example of Christ is done wholly by the power of Another. He said "not my will, but thine," and was ready to hold to this when the following of the will of God seemed to mean failure. There is the danger that Christian workers to-day, lured by the example of the success of the children of the world in their undertakings, will go after the same sort of great, showy results in the eyes of men, in their spiritual matters. This is not after the mind of Christ, but partakes of that other mind which says "I WILL." The mind of Christ will care for no results except those that are the product of the Spirit. And in securing these the eyes will not be upon results but upon the Master, to seek his will in every matter of service, leaving with him the results and the rewards.

Defilement of the Spirit

The third danger, most subtle of all, and pervading all, is pride, the exaltation of the human. And this is the temptation that Satan often successfully uses upon the spiritual Christian who has gotten beyond serving in the energy of the flesh or in the energy of the soul. We must cleanse ourselves of all defilement of flesh *and of spirit*. Serving "in lowliness of mind, each counting other better than himself,"—this is to have the mind of Christ. Serving in love that envieth not, that vaunteth not itself, is not puffed up, that *seeketh not its own*,—this is to have the mind of Christ. It is at the other pole from pride.

How are we to have the mind of Christ? Not by looking at him as an example and trying to imitate him. There is real hopelessness in singing

> Trying to walk in the steps of the Saviour,
>
> Trying to follow our Saviour and King,
>
> Shaping our lives by his blessed example....

For that is just what we cannot do—shape our lives by his example. When we are ready to stop "trying" to do this, and will yield ourselves that we may be conformed to his death, then our trying may be changed to trusting, we can "leave the miracle to him," and returning to the beautiful hymn whose first verse makes a bad start, we can sing with new meaning the opening lines of the third verse:

> Walking by faith in the steps of our Saviour,
>
> Upward, still upward, we'll follow our Guide.

THE SECOND COMING AND VICTORY

THE next great event in God's program for the redemption of the world is the coming again to the earth of the Lord Jesus Christ. The last chapter of the Old Testament points forward to his second coming. The last recorded words of the Lord Jesus are his words of promise, "Surely, I come quickly," in the last chapter of the New Testament. The last recorded prayer of God's people in the Word is the answer of their heart to this promise, "Even so come, Lord Jesus."

The last word of the Old Testament is the word "curse,"—"lest I come and smite the earth with a curse." The central word of the last verse in the New Testament is "grace." He will come with the judgments of his curse and with the revelation of his grace.

Are You Ready for His Coming?

Among the many signs that seem to point to the nearness of his coming there is none more striking than the movement of the Spirit in separating the children of God from the things of the world and making them hungry for the things of eternity. There are many sad evidences of falling away, and of increasing worldliness on the part of large masses of professing Christians, but these make all the more notable that deep hunger for victory in Christ and conformity to his likeness which increasing numbers of Christians are sharing. Is this the work of the Spirit in making a little flock ready for his coming? Are *you* ready?

The coming of Christ is the great incentive to holiness that is held before Christians in the New Testament. "Every one that hath this hope [the hope of his coming] set on him [set on Jesus] purifieth himself, even as he is pure" (1 John 3:3).

There are many motives by which the Lord lovingly urges us to seek complete victory in him. We long for a life of joy and peace that we do not have. We long to be rid of a life of struggle against "besetting sins." Or we are eager to have power in service and get results for Christ that are largely absent in our experience. By this or that motive the Spirit leads us to an earnest seeking of God's secret of the life of faith. But beyond all these motives is that supreme desire to be well pleasing to the Lord Jesus Christ, who loved us and gave himself for us. "And now, little children, abide in him; that, when he shall appear, we may have boldness, and not be ashamed before him at his coming" (1 John 2:28).

Boldness Before Him Then and Now

The one way to be ready for his coming, to have boldness and not to be ashamed, is to abide in him. "Whosoever abideth in him sinneth not" (1 John

3:6); to be cleansed from sin and to abide in that cleansing makes us ready for his coming. If we are not enjoying the Victorious Life, which is just another way of saying "abiding life," we are not ready for his coming. And if we are not ready for his personal coming, we are not ready for his presence in our midst now. That which gives us boldness *then* is what gives us boldness before his throne *now* when we come to pray. "Beloved, if our heart condemn us not, we have boldness toward God: and whatsoever we ask we receive of him, because we keep his commandments and do the things that are pleasing in his sight ... and he that keepeth his commandments abideth in him, and he in him" (1 John 3:21, 22, 24).

If the coming of the Lord is in God's Word linked so vitally with a life of personal holiness, it is essential that Christians should understand what the Spirit has revealed to us concerning the truth of his coming. It is only at our peril that we neglect it. It is not an accident that most of those who are rejoicing in the Victorious Life are or become deeply interested in the truths of the Word concerning Christ's coming.

But how shall we know whether our view of his Second Coming is the Scriptural view?

Testing Our View of His Coming

There are two tests that will show with certainty to what extent our belief about Christ's coming is a vital heart belief such as the Apostles had. The first test concerns more definitely our personal relation to his coming. Is the hope of his coming a real hope for you that makes it the incentive to be ready and makes it a real event to watch for with expectation, as for the return of a loved one?

The second test relates to the whole sweep of God's purposes of redemption and the part that Christ's Second Coming plays in them. A right understanding at this point will determine the general plan of activities of the Church of Christ and of the individual Christian in this present day of Grace. How essential then to know God's thought on this subject, and how idle to suggest that this truth is not of practical bearing on present service. Both the spirit of service and the scope of service are involved, and these two tests show how intensely practical and necessary is the right view of his coming.

The first test has already been considered, and it is seen that the Victorious Life truth is vitally linked with the hope of his coming. The second test of our belief regarding his coming is even more fundamental, and again it will be seen to be closely tied up with the heart secret of the Victorious Life, and with the truth of regeneration as well.

It is a common thing to speak of the doctrine of Christ's Second Coming as of greater or less relative importance than certain other doctrines; thus, it is pointed out that the Second Coming is mentioned more often in the New Testament than any other doctrine except that of the atonement. It leads to confusion thus to speak of the teachings of the Word as though they could be divided. While it is convenient to study the doctrines separately we miss a great truth if we fail to remember that all these teachings brought to us by the Word of God are connected one with the other and together form a complete unity.

The Second Coming Necessary to the Atonement

The doctrine of Christ's Second Coming is not a teaching apart from the atonement, but is *necessary to the atonement.* That is, God's plan of redemption for us cannot be completed apart from the coming of Christ and the events connected with that coming. His coming therefore is essential to salvation. Not that the understanding of the doctrine is essential to individual salvation. A sinner needs to know very little Scripture in order to be saved; when the Spirit has convicted him of sin a single sentence of Glad Tidings will suffice. But it requires the whole redemptive purposes of God to make that salvation possible. And those redemptive purposes include the appearing a second time of the God-man, our Lord Jesus Christ. The importance of our Lord's Second Coming, then, is exactly parallel with the importance of his first coming and of his present ministry for the believer.

The Word of God presents salvation in a threefold aspect. There is the past, the present, and the future of salvation. "We were saved; we are being saved; we shall be saved."

The Three "Appearings"

On every side these three aspects of salvation are emphasized in the Word. Attention has frequently been called to the three appearings mentioned in the ninth chapter of Hebrews: "*now to appear* in the presence of God for us ... now once in the end of the world *hath he appeared* to put away sin by the sacrifice of himself ... and unto them that look for him *shall he appear* the second time without sin unto salvation" (Heb. 9:24, 26, 28).

In the three Shepherd Psalms the same truth is shadowed forth. The twenty-second Psalm points to the redemption accomplished on Calvary, and is the Psalm of crucifixion and resurrection; the twenty-third Psalm is a picture of the present resurrection life in Christ; and in the twenty-fourth Psalm we have the picture of the coming King. He is seen in these three Psalms as the Good Shepherd who laid down his life for the sheep; as the Great Shepherd who rose again from the dead, who makes us perfect "in every good thing to do his will, working in us that which is well-pleasing in his sight" (Heb. 13:20, 21); and as the Chief Shepherd who will appear to give the crown of glory to his faithful servants (1 Peter 5:4).

This threefold salvation is sometimes spoken of as justification, sanctification, and glorification: first, salvation from the penalty of sin; second, salvation from the power of sin; and third, salvation from the possibility of sin.

There are three fundamental errors by which Satan seeks to rob of its power this threefold Gospel, the grace of the Lord Jesus Christ in his past, present, and future work.

Discounting Christ's Past Work

There is the teaching that we are saved from the death penalty of our sins by Christ plus our own effort. This error finds expression in many ways. One mistake, more common in the past generation than to-day, is to consider it presumptuous to be sure of salvation. Now if the work is wholly Christ's it cannot be presumptuous to be certain that that work is complete and is satisfactory to the Father. Then there is the belief that salvation from death and hell depends on our holding on to Christ, and since we may fail and thus fall away, we are never entirely sure of salvation until death comes or until the Lord comes to claim us. These teachings present a subtle *mixture of works and grace*. If we are saved by grace, if redemption is entirely the work of Christ, then may we indeed have assurance of eternal salvation. In its extreme form this error is pure paganism, salvation by our own efforts. In its more refined and moderate form it keeps Christians from the glorious present assurance of their eternal safety in the Lord Jesus. The safeguard against all these errors is to remember that salvation from the penalty of sin is all of grace. And grace means, Jesus Christ did it all for me. If he did, the work is finished, the work is perfect, and we have a sure guarantee that the purposes of God will be carried out. No one can pluck the saved soul out of the Father's hand.

Discounting His Present Work

Most Christians are clear on the truth that they are saved by grace. They make no effort of their own to add to the perfect atonement that Christ has made for their sins. But these same Christians when facing the present tense of salvation, the second part of the threefold Gospel, declare that here our own efforts are necessary. We must co-operate with God in fighting sin. We are justified by faith, but we are sanctified, gradually, by struggle. Their error is that they are *mixing works and grace*. God's plan for present salvation from the power of sin is exactly the same as his plan for deliverance from the penalty of sin. It is all of grace.

The test of the truth of our view as to Christ's Second Coming and the future tense of our salvation is as infallibly certain as the tests of the other aspects of salvation. For salvation is all of grace, and any view which makes salvation for the individual or for the universe a mixture of God's work and man's work, a mixture of God's grace and man's effort, is in error.

The Two Views of Our Lord's Return

There are two views of our Lord's coming. One is that the Church of Christ through the preaching of the Gospel and by co-operating with other agencies for righteousness, will Christianize the social order and bring in the period of righteousness which the Bible pictures as the Kingdom age. At the close of this period, the Lord Jesus will come to judge the world. This is called the post-millennial view, because the Kingdom age is known as the "millennium," or the thousand years. The other view is that this thousand years of blessedness, or the Kingdom age, will not be inaugurated until Christ himself comes as King to set up the new order on earth. This is known as the pre-millennial view.

A well known Christian leader who has been very active in the preaching and working for "social regeneration," gave a message on the task of the Church in the present world crisis, and the problem of the Church in making the world what it ought to be. He announced as his text, "And he that sitteth on the throne said, Behold, I make all things new" (Rev. 21:5). One who heard the message remarked that the speaker after announcing his text, "with two swift kicks kicked the text out of the auditorium, and did not allow it to enter again during his discourse." For the opening sentence of his message was this: "Can we, the followers of the Lord Jesus Christ, make things over?"

God's Word does not say, "we, the followers of the Lord Jesus." It says "I"; and the Son of God sitting on the throne of his glory is the speaker. The Word of God does not speak of making things over. It says, "Behold, I make all things *new*."

Discounting Christ's Future Work

Here is the fundamental error of the post-millennial view of the Lord's coming: *it is a mixture of works and grace.*

God's plan for establishing righteousness in the universe is exactly the same as his plan for establishing righteousness in the human heart. It is all of grace, not of works. The pre-millennial view means the Kingdom age by grace, as the Victorious Life means the Kingdom principles in the individual heart by grace.

Let each Christian earnestly face these two tests of his attitude toward the coming of the Lord Jesus Christ.

Make the Blessed Hope a Vital Power!

If his hope of the coming of the Lord is not an incentive of vital and present power in his life, there is something wrong with his theory. If a Christian believes that it is not possible for the Lord to come for at least a thousand years, or until the period during which Satan is bound has run its course (whether a thousand literal years or not), can he honestly say that the blessed hope of the personal appearing of his Lord is a vital power in the life?

The second test of our view of his coming can apply also to every part of our salvation. Have we the blessed assurance of eternal salvation through the blood that gives us eagerness and power to lead others into the same assurance? Are we rejoicing in all the blessed "present tenses of salvation," victory by grace through faith? Are we surrounded by his own light in these dark days because we know that the world's problem is to be solved by grace, by God himself, so that we live "soberly, righteously, and godly in this present age; looking for that blessed hope, and the glorious appearing of the great God and our Saviour Jesus Christ"?

CHRISTIAN SCIENCE AND VICTORY

CHRISTIAN SCIENCE offers a life of freedom from worry or anxiety. It proposes to give the secret of the smiling face in the midst of any sort of circumstances.

Christian Science offers complete freedom from the dominion of sin.

Christian Science offers to make faith a vital and all-pervading force in daily life.

Christian Science offers to give deliverance from the bondage of sickness.

It is not wise for Christians to attempt to meet Christian Science by ridicule and sarcasm. Christian Science is offering to supply exactly the things that the hearts of thousands of church members are craving. It is not strange that many should be investigating its claims. If the indication in a single Christian Science center is a fair criterion, there are thousands of church members daily looking into this supposed "new" teaching to see if they can find a faith with a vital reality in it.

These things that Christian Science claims to supply are just the things that are offered to every Christian through the sufficient grace of the Lord Jesus.

The Victorious Life in Christ is a life kept free from worry or anxiety. Its possessors have the secret of a constant, abiding joy that is independent of circumstances (Phil. 4:6, 7; John 15:11; 16:22).

The Victorious Life, which is just Christ himself in the believer, gives complete victory over sin, without struggle (Rom. 6:14; 1 Cor. 10:13; John 8:36).

The Victorious Life is the life of faith, walking in the Spirit, looking unto Jesus, enduring as seeing him who is invisible, counting the unseen things the eternal and real things (Col. 3:3; Gal. 2:20; John 15:7).

The Victorious Life is a life of prosperity for body as well as for spirit, for in Christ is the supply of every present need, for body, soul, and spirit (3 John 2; Ps. 103:3; Matt. 8:17; Rom. 8:11).

If the fulness of the blessing of the Gospel of Christ were faithfully preached there would be little prepared soil among church members for the springing up of the seeds of "Christian Science." It is the Enemy who is sowing these seeds and the supreme sign of his subtle work is this apparent likeness to the true grain. What is the fundamental distinction between Christian Science and the Victorious Life in Christ, between God's truth and Satan's imitation of that truth?

Error's Imitations of Truth

Christian Science says: "In nothing be anxious: there is nothing to be anxious about. All troubles are creations of the mind, results of wrong thinking, and the cure for them is to think them away."

The Word of God says, "In nothing be anxious." Not because there is nothing to be anxious about. There is. There is that which required the bloody sweat of the Son of God in Gethsemane. But the Word of God tells us that full provision has been made for those wrong things that may well cause anxiety. Back of the word of the Spirit in Philippians, "In nothing be anxious," is God. Back of the Christian Science word is "mortal mind."

Christian Science says, "Reckon yourselves dead unto sin: because sin has no real existence, and since it is a creation of the wrong thinking of mortal mind, the way to think it out of existence is to reckon yourself dead to it. As you reckon, as you believe, you are dead to sin, and for you it has no reality or existence."

Faith Does Not Create Facts

The Word of God says, "Reckon ye also yourselves to be dead indeed unto sin." Not because sin does not exist. It does. Not because sin is not real. There is nothing more real in the universe. But Jesus Christ has met the full measure of the guilt and penalty and pollution of sin, and has completely conquered it. If we are crucified with him, buried with him and risen again with him, as every child of God is, then we are to reckon it true that we are dead unto sin: not because our thinking can change facts, but because God himself tells us to count on a great fact, something that he himself has accomplished; as we reckon that fact true our faith is laying hold of the benefits in present experience of that redemption which God has accomplished. *My faith does not make the fact true.* Faith gives me the benefit of a fact that is true whether I believe it or not. True faith is impossible without something real to rest upon. Satan's counterfeit faith in Christian Science returns upon itself, endeavors to create facts by thinking them true.

Christian Science says that sickness and death are delusions of the mortal mind. It does not offer a scheme of healing disease but a philosophy to make clear that disease does not exist except as an error in the thinking of mortal mind. Clear away that error in thinking, and the effects of the so-called sickness will disappear.

The Word of God says, "The wages of sin is *death*"; and, "Himself took our infirmities, and bare our *sicknesses.*" Without entering here into the question of the use of remedies, or the limitations to the use of "the prayer of faith" which will heal the sick, let us remember that in Christ there is full provision for sin *and all its results*. He came to destroy the works of the devil. It is certainly God's highest and first will that his children should be in health of body, not in sickness, if this result can be had without injuring his children in other ways. God's permission of sickness and premature death among his devoted children must not be pointed to as an indication that it is not his first will that all his children should enjoy health of body. God would have all men to be saved, and has made full provision for their salvation: but not all are saved; God would have all his children abide continually in Christ and be kept from sinning, and he has made complete provision for this: but few are entering into their full privileges of victory; God would have his children free from disease, for he is the God who forgives all our iniquities and heals all our diseases, and in Christ he has made full and complete provision for this: but in his infinite love and wisdom he permits many of his children to continue in suffering of body for longer or shorter periods.

Christian Science Kills Faith

In this contrast between Christian Science and the Word of God it will be seen that the teachings of this "faith" cult make faith impossible. Satan always strikes at the center of things in his attacks on Christians and on the Word of God; so he takes away their faith and that which it rests upon. Again and again in personal interviews with those seeking victory, when the meaning of faith has been explained the answer has come, "Why, that would be just like Christian Science. I cannot make a thing true just by believing it." With Christian Science, thinking a thing true makes it true, or rather, "thinking right" removes the error which has resulted only because the thinking has been wrong. But real faith rests always on facts. We believe, not in order to make a fact true, but because it is true.

So startling is the parallel between what Christian Science offers and what the Victorious Life in Christ guarantees, that a number who have read articles in *The Sunday School Times* have written to ask if the Victorious Life teaching and Christian Science were not practically the same. In answer to these inquiries a brief Open Letter was published a few years ago pointing out the difference between Christian Science and "the Victorious Life." The Open Letter closed with this sentence: "They differ from each other as do food and poison, noon-day and midnight, omnipotence and impotence, life and death, Heaven and hell, Christ and Satan."

A Christian Science Leader's Admission

A leading advocate of Christian Science called upon the Editor of *The Sunday School Times* to protest against this article. The interesting thing about the interview with this cultured representative of Christian Science was his earnest effort to prove that he and his fellow Scientists believed just what Christians who were teaching the Victorious Life believed, and were aiming at the same kind of life. As each point was mentioned there was this apparent agreement, until—mark this—until the vicarious atonement through the blood of the Lord Jesus Christ was mentioned. There he frankly confessed that they parted company; they do not accept any atonement for sin.

At a Victorious Life Conference a Christian Scientist girl was prevailed upon to attend a meeting where the subject was the meaning of faith in laying hold of God's Word that "My grace is sufficient for thee," and similar words of fact and promise. At the close of the meeting an opportunity was given for those who wished by rising to commit the whole matter of victory to God, trusting him to do it all by grace. To the astonishment of her friends, the Christian Scientist girl rose. She asked them, "Are you surprised that I stood? That is what I have believed all along." She was accepting it all as good Christian Science. At the close of the period of question and discussion the speaker asked if there were those present who had never accepted the Lord Jesus as Saviour from sin, and did not know salvation through the shed blood of Jesus. At the mention of the blood of the Lord Jesus Christ, this young woman who had stood up to take a step of faith for victory, rose at once from her seat and left the room.

Here we come to the heart of Christian Science error: it denies the blood, the vicarious atonement for sin. And here is the secret of many unsatisfactory attempts on the part of Christians to live a life of victory. Earnestly seeking to claim the wonderful promises of God's word, many have failed to understand the meaning of the blood of Christ and to share in experience his crucifixion death, that they might also know the resurrection victory.

A Masterpiece of Imitation Victory

Christian Science is the devil's great masterpiece of imitation victory. It is the vain attempt to know the resurrection life without the crucifixion death. It is the attempted robbery of the life pictured in the twenty-third Psalm, the life of still waters and green pastures, the life in which all the needs of the sheep are met by an all-powerful and all-loving Shepherd. But while attempting to claim the twenty-third Psalm, the Christian Scientist blots out the twenty-second Psalm with its agony of Calvary and its resurrection victory. We must be one with the Lord Jesus in his death and burial before we can be one with him in resurrection life. The blood of the Lord Jesus must be kept always at the heart of the teaching and the experience of the Victorious Life. The reason for much disappointment in the living of the Victorious Life is because there is what may be called a Christian Science acceptance of the teaching without a real foundation being laid in the blood of the Lamb.

First of all, the foundation must be laid in a clear understanding of the meaning of the new birth. Those who have had experience in dealing with hungry Christians seeking the life of victory in Christ, have been amazed at the number of such earnest inquirers who have no clear conception of what it means to be born again, or to be saved by grace.

Can You Tell a Sinner Just How to Be Saved?

The following question has been put again and again to audiences consisting of Christian workers and Bible students: "How many here are sure you could tell an inquirer exactly what he must do to become a Christian and receive the new birth?" The result of this question is nothing less than startling. As many as half and two-thirds in these audiences have not raised their hands to indicate that they could explain the way of salvation. But if one cannot tell an inquirer how to be saved, neither can he tell why he himself is sure of salvation. And until one knows the word regarding the real meaning of sin and the atonement, there will be only disappointment in trying to get hold of the experience of victory in Christ.

The steps of salvation are perfectly simple. First, one must know that he is lost. Otherwise he cannot need a Saviour. To believe that the Lord Jesus Christ died in my place, I must believe that I am such a sinner as deserved death. "All have sinned and come short of the glory of God" (Rom. 3:23). Joined with this is the word, "The wages of sin is death; but the free gift of God is eternal life in Christ Jesus our Lord" (Rom. 6:23). I am saved by grace through faith (Eph. 2:8); faith is believing that all my sins were put on Jesus and he paid the penalty for them (Isa. 53:6); now I have been born again and am a child of God; and I know it not because I feel it, but because God's Word says so (John 1:12; 1 John 5:9-13).

A clear understanding of the blood will save us from a superficial idea of sin and its awfulness. If the cross of Christ is ever in view we shall have God's estimate of sin, and there will be a clear realization that it required the whole sacrifice of Calvary to accomplish the miracle of victory. In a testimony meeting at a Victorious Life conference a Christian was explaining that his chief difficulty had been with "those little troubles," such as irritation, impatience, pride and such things. "You mean those devilish sins," the leader of the meeting suggested. There is not likely to be that earnest, agonizing heart cry, "O wretched man that I am! who shall deliver me from the body of this death," so long as we think of sin as little troubles to be overcome. All sin is devilish, and the Son of God is the only one who has won the victory over sin. Victory for us then begins with the cross of Christ, but it is possible only as we keep continually under that shed blood and appropriating His resurrection life. The whole sacrifice of Calvary is necessary to keep us free from the least of what we call the little sins.

Christian Science not only would rob a Christian of faith, it would rob him of the blessed hope. "The second appearing of Jesus is unquestionably the spiritual advent of the advancing idea of God in Christian Science," says Mrs.

Eddy. Hope points toward the future, and Christian Science has no place for future deliverance from evil and sin, except as the human race learns that these are errors of mortal mind.

It Takes Away Faith, Hope, Love

Christian Science would rob us of love. It is a startling fact that not a dollar is given by Scientists to preach the Gospel among those who have never heard the name of Jesus. They have no foreign missionary societies. A Christian who had spent fifteen years in work among the poor and degraded classes in New York City was rebuked by a Christian Scientist for suggesting that her faith was not the faith of the Bible; he asked her why it was that in his fifteen years' experience, touching all phases of work for the relief of the destitute in body and spirit in New York, he had never come across a single Christian Scientist helping in the work. She had no answer. It is a religion without compassion.

Faith, hope, and love are linked together in a remarkable passage in Hebrews 10:19-25. Close to the word faith is mention of "the blood of Jesus"; not far from "hope" are the words "so much the more as ye see the day drawing nigh"; and in close conjunction with "love" is "good works." Thus are these great foundation stones of the Christian Faith linked in the Word of God. All of them are denied, and are made impossible by Christian Science.

The antidote to Christian Science is the Word of God. But do they not found their belief on the Bible? No. The Bible is not necessary to Christian Science. Indeed, it is one of the great handicaps to the system. Not many Scientists are as honest, or as well informed, as the locomotive engineer who recently explained that Christian Scientists knew that the Bible was not true, and that men would gradually give it up; but it had such a hold on people that no religion could hope to have a hearing unless it professed to be founded on the Bible. When people get hold of the truth of Christian Science, they will see, he added, that the Bible is not needed and is false; the purpose of Christian Science is to lead people away from the error of the Bible. That is certainly the purpose of the real founder of Christian Science, whether or not it was in the mind of the woman he used to propagate the cult.

And the antidote to superficial views of the Victorious Life, which partake of these errors of Christian Science, is the Word of God. Feed on it, meditate on it *day and night*. So will the living Word continue to be your Life, guarding and keeping you in that victory which is Christ.

IS IT A "SECOND BLESSING"?

"DO you believe in the second blessing?"

"To be sure I do," answered a Christian whose reply voices the judgment of many, "but I shouldn't confine it to a second blessing. I believe in hundreds of blessings after conversion." Whatever may be our view of such a term as "the second blessing," let us not lose the experience it describes by confusing these hundreds of blessings with that distinct change which comes in a life when the secret of complete victory is learned.

A noted Christian leader in England who was prejudiced against the teaching of a "higher life" was prevailed upon to hear a message on the subject. He approached the speaker, who was a friend of his, with this criticism: "That is all well enough, but you are preaching lop-sided truth. What we need is all-round truth." "Yes," was the reply, "but we are preaching to lop-sided Christians. When we get them into the center then we can give them all-round truth."

Dr. Griffith Thomas, who relates this incident of the English preachers, has pointed out that "the perfecting of the saints" means literally "the adjusting of the saints." It is as when a broken shoulder needs to be set before the blood can flow properly and the arm be used. It is this adjustment of "lop-sided Christians" which marks the great change. Those who experience the change realize that it is something different from any blessing they have received since conversion, and different from any new experience of deepening that will come in the life later.

What is this distinct change that comes in the life of the Christian?

It is clear that the Scriptures never hold before the believer two *standards* for the Christian life. The New Testament does recognize that Christians may walk as "carnal," whereas their true state is to be spiritual (Gal. 6:1; 1 Cor. 3:1). It recognizes that Christians may walk after the flesh or after the Spirit (Rom. 8:4; Gal. 5:16).

A Spirit-Filled Life God's Only Standard

But this does not mean that there are two standards for Christians to choose between. On the contrary, the Word makes plain that when a Christian walks after the flesh, when he is "carnal," he is acting as though he were not a child of God at all. "And I brethren, could not speak unto you as unto spiritual, but as unto carnal, as unto babes in Christ. I fed you with milk, not with meat; for ye were not yet able to bear it: nay, not even now are ye able; for ye are yet carnal: for whereas there is among you jealousy and strife, are ye not carnal, and do ye not walk after the manner of men?" These Christians,

Paul says, were walking as natural men, who have not been born again, instead of living as spiritual children of God.

There is no platform below the Spirit-filled life which affords a safe resting ground for a Christian. One who calls himself by the name of Christ, but does not have the fulness of the Spirit, and yet says that he has no desire for this deeper experience, is confessing that there is no evidence he has ever been born again. For while a Christian may live below the standard Christ desires he cannot be comfortable in doing it; the Spirit of God within him is longing for the driving out of everything contrary to the life of Christ.

The heart of the Spirit-filled life is freedom from sin. A normal Christian is a man who does not sin. "We who died to sin, how shall we any longer live therein?" (Rom. 6:2). "These things write I unto you that ye may not sin" (1 John 2:1). "Whosoever is begotten of God doeth no sin" (1 John 3:9). "We know that whosoever is begotten of God sinneth not" (1 John 5:18).

Some teachers who have noted these plain statements of the Word have concluded that a Christian does not commit sin, and that so soon as a Christian does he ceases to be a Christian. If he is sinning it is a proof that he is not a Christian, and will not be reinstated as a child of God till he ceases his sinning. These teachers, however, see the difficulty that in the heart of many Christians are wrong feelings that should not be there, and which they do not want there but over which they apparently have no control. To get over this and other difficulties they explain that a Christian does not *commit* "outward" sins, though he has these sinful impulses in his heart. Even this standard, it is to be feared, would cut down the number of Christians to a small minimum.

A Normal Christian is Free from Sin

But a more serious objection to this method of explaining these difficult verses in First John is that it contradicts the very point that the Apostle is making. If close attention is paid to the conclusion of First John 3:9 it should guard from these errors: "Whosoever is begotten of God doeth no sin, because his seed abideth in him: and *he cannot sin*, because he is begotten of God."

That seed which is born of God is, as Dr. A. J. Ramsey has pointed out, the Child of God himself, not a seed *in* him. While he abides he cannot sin. (As Moffatt also translates: "The offspring of God remain in Him.") The whole argument of the Epistle of John, and particularly of this portion, is that a normal Christian is one who is free from sin. The Apostle does not mean to say that a child of God does not "deliberately" sin, or that he does not "continue in sin" as the rule of his life, or that he does not let the inward impulses of sin express themselves: he means that the Christian, while he abides in Christ, where he belongs, does not sin. He is God's new creation, and walks in the light having fellowship with God. For "God is light, and in him is no darkness at all" (1 John 1:5).

When a Christian Acts as a Child of Satan

Does John mean that a Christian does not sin, or that he ceases to be a Christian if he sins? The opposite is taught in this very Epistle. John is writing these things that Christians may not sin, but he recognizes that they may, and tells them just what to do to have the sin cleansed away in case they do sin.

When a Christian sins, *he is acting against his true nature*. That is the argument of First John and of all the Epistles. When a Christian sins, he is acting *as though he were* a child of the devil. He as a child of God can have nothing to do with sin. But there is his free will to step out of the place of abiding, and this makes possible the tragedy of a Christian's sinning.

James is facing this tragedy of a Christian's acting against his true nature when he exclaims: "Doth the fountain send forth from the same opening sweet water and bitter? can a fig tree, my brethren, yield olives, or a vine figs? neither can salt water yield sweet" (James 3:10-12). All these things act according to their true nature. If a Christian acted thus there would flow always from his life and lips the fruit of the Spirit. But the Apostle shows in the passage that a Christian may pray with the same mouth that he uses to say mean things about his neighbor, and that he may have in his heart "bitter jealousy and faction."

Here, then, is our foundation truth that God has but one standard for the Christian life, one kind of holiness, and that is the standard of his Son, who is to be our life. And that Life, that holiness, God has given *to every Christian*.

God's Perfect Provision for Every Christian

It was to those "carnal" Corinthians, who had jealousy and strife in their midst, that Paul by the Spirit wrote: "I thank my God always concerning you, for the grace of God which was given you in Christ Jesus; that in everything ye were enriched in him, in all utterance and all knowledge; even as the testimony of Christ was confirmed in you: so that ye come behind in no gift; waiting for the revelation of our Lord Jesus Christ; who shall also confirm you unto the end, that ye may be unreprovable in the day of our Lord Jesus Christ. God is faithful, through whom ye were called into the fellowship of his Son Jesus Christ our Lord" (1 Cor. 1:4-9).

This surely is a picture of the fulness of blessing in Christ, and it is stated that this grace had been given to the Corinthians because they were Christians. Similarly in the eighth chapter of Romans the life of victory is described: "For the law of the Spirit of life in Christ Jesus made me free from the law of sin and of death" (Rom. 8:2). This freedom belongs to every believer in the Lord Jesus. So throughout the New Testament it is made clear that when God spared not his own Son but delivered him up for us all, he freely gave with Christ all things that a Christian needs.

But while there is but one salvation, and one plan of salvation, this salvation has a two-fold aspect. God has indeed only one standard for Christians, the standard of his Son, that is complete holiness. But God's message of salvation comes to two distinct classes of people, to lost sinners, and to saints—sinners saved by grace.

Christians Need to Be Saved

"If while we were enemies we were reconciled to God through the death of his Son" (Rom. 5:10). This is the message of salvation for sinners. The next words of this verse are very significant: "Much more." The apostle has just been speaking of salvation for sinners, and now he is to tell us something "much more." This word should prepare us for some amazing revelation of his grace. "Much more, being reconciled, shall we be saved by his life."

Do Christians, then, need salvation? Indeed they do, and the Word of God suggests here that a good name for that salvation which reconciled Christian needs is "the much more salvation," and this is just another way of saying "the Victorious Life."

God has granted that life to every Christian. But not every Christian is enjoying it. For the Christian has the terrible power of choosing to walk after the flesh and not after the Spirit. God's plan is that the Christian life should be a moment by moment miracle life, just as the new birth is a miracle. "If we live by the Spirit, by the Spirit let us also walk" (Gal. 5:25). Being born again, and "walking," are two distinct things. When a Christian learns that God intends him to walk by faith, letting Christ do it all, just as he has believed that Christ has done it all in the matter of saving him from the penalty of his sins, then the Christian is ready to enter into the fulness of the Spirit, which is the Victorious Life.

And when he does enter by faith for the first time into this complete victory, which has been his privilege all along in Christ, there is such a marked change that it is natural for a Christian to think of it as a "second blessing." There is that perfectly clear distinction between being born again, and "walking" or living moment by moment after the new birth has taken place. The man who has been born again is in a place to take hold of the much-more salvation for Christians as he could not do in his unregenerate state.

Testing Our "Doctrine" of Victory

There are some simple tests of our "view" of complete victory over sin which will show whether we are in danger of coming into bondage to a *doctrine*.

Any view that centers attention upon self is dangerous. The heart secret of victory is looking away from self unto Christ. If I testify, "I am holy"; if I must look into my own state, examining self to see whether this holiness still remains, I am on wrong ground.

Any view that brings into prominence my past record of victory or holiness leads to difficulties. The testimony, "I have not sinned for so many weeks or months since my new experience" may be given with sincerity, and the speaker may intend to give the glory to God. Nevertheless, it is a wrong testimony, and no encouragement is given in the Word for such a statement. For one thing, no human being has a perfect memory; none of us can have accurate knowledge of past states of consciousness. Victory is always a matter of the present moment, and if we are occupied with Christ and *his* perfect work for us, the matter of *our* past record is of no consequence, so far as it bears on present victory by faith.

Any view that centers attention upon feeling is on the wrong basis. Many Christians who have come into the new experience of the fulness of the Spirit have been overwhelmed with flood-tides of blessed feeling. In some cases this exalted state of feeling has continued for weeks or months. Some have counted this the "witness of the Spirit" that a new work of grace has been wrought in their hearts. Many have been thrown into confusion and darkness by waiting for this "witness of the Spirit," which they have been taught to believe is some wondrous consciousness in their feeling. Others who have had such a "witness" have later lost the feeling and have wondered whether their experience has gone. God often permits the feeling to go, that his child may learn to look to Christ and to the fact of his grace in the life, rather than to the feelings, which vary according to temperament and circumstances.

What is the "Witness of the Spirit"?

Feeling or emotion should not be discounted, but should be kept in its right place. Praise God for every blessed emotion that is of his Spirit, but praise him also when the emotion is entirely absent. He and his grace remain the same, while the feelings go up and down. There should be, indeed, a continuous consciousness of his presence, but consciousness is based on fact and is not to be confused with emotion.

As to the "witness of the Spirit," there is no suggestion in the Word of God that this "witness" has any connection with a great flood-tide of feeling. "He that believeth on the Son of God hath the witness in him: he that believeth not God hath made him a liar; because he hath not believed in the witness that God hath borne concerning his Son. And the witness is this, that God gave unto us eternal life, and this life is in his Son" (1 John 5:10, 11). The witness is God's record, or God's eternal Word to us, that he has done something, that he has given us a gift. He does not want us to *feel* this word, or witness of his. He wants us to *believe* it. One who does not believe it makes God a liar, and this is what Christians are in danger of doing, both in regard to salvation from the penalty of sin and salvation from the power of sin. When we believe this word, and the wonder of the gift breaks upon us more and more, we shall have feelings, of course, and they will find expression according to our different temperaments and environments.

(Dr. Griffith Thomas notes that the often abused passage on the witness of the Spirit in Romans eight does not say that the Spirit beareth witness *to* our spirit, but *with* our spirit, that we are children of God. That is, our spirit says "Father," and the Holy Spirit says "Father" with us.)

John Wesley on Use of Terms

Whatever our "view," let us guard against laying emphasis upon certain terms, and making these the test of correctness. We should remember that God has granted the same experience to Christians who have come into their experience by different paths and who therefore explain it in different ways. The important thing, after all, is to have the fruits of the experience in the life. John Wesley, who had the experience, whatever our view of his theology, has a word of wise counsel at this point:

"Beware of tempting others to separate from you. Give no offense which can possibly be avoided; see that your practice be in all things suitable to your profession, adorning the doctrine of God our Saviour. Be particularly careful in speaking of yourself; you may not indeed deny the work of God; but speak of it when you are called thereto in the most inoffensive manner possible. Avoid all magnificent, pompous words. Indeed, you need give it no general name; neither 'perfection,' 'sanctification,' 'the second blessing,' nor 'the having attained.' Rather speak of the particulars that God has wrought for you.... And answer any other plain question that is asked with modesty and simplicity."

Was It Sin, or "Infirmity"?

Any view that leads us to lower the standard of holiness to fit our experience, or to argue with the devil or with ourselves over sin, is in error. A Christian who has had a blessed new experience notices something in the life that is not quite according to the Spirit of Christ. He begins to examine it and decides that this is not a sin but one of the "infirmities" from which he has not expected complete deliverance. Or he confesses it as a sin and is cleansed in the blood of Christ, but since he does not want to believe that he has lost his experience he explains that this was a temptation from without and was not due to any evil within. Or, not able to delude himself with these bits of human reasonings, he falls back into his old life of struggle and failure.

John Wesley has a word in season here also: "And if any of you should at any time fall from what you now are, if you should again feel pride or unbelief, or any temper from which you are now delivered, do not deny it, do not hide it, do not disguise it at all, at the peril of your soul. At all events, go to one in whom you can confide, and speak just what you feel. God will enable him to speak a word in season which shall be health to your soul. And surely the Lord will again lift up your head and cause the bones that have been broken to rejoice."

The Bible treatment of the conquest of sin is subject to none of these distressing difficulties. It guards from dangerous errors on every side, and at the same time leaves no loopholes for tolerating sin as do the current views held by nearly all Christians.

What Terms Does the Bible Use?

God says, "Reckon ye also yourselves to be dead unto sin" (Rom. 6:11). There are two ways the devil would like us to interpret this. One is by his old lie regarding "death." He wants us to believe that the capacity for sinning is taken away so that we shall not acknowledge sin to be sin, and shall call the works of the devil the fruit of the Spirit. But death is not annihilation, but separation. It is not that some "thing" within us has been put out of existence. All that we were as lost sinners, in our unregenerate state—the "old man"—was crucified with Christ and is buried, and a Christian is to reckon that fact true. But he is to remember that there is ever the possibility of turning our members over as instruments of sin. And whenever sin enters, when anything in thought, word or deed that is contrary to the Spirit of Christ has a place in the life, it means that self is on the throne and we are alive to sin.

But Satan's other interpretation of this verse is his favorite one, for by it he deludes most Christians. It is only when this fails that he tries the other and drives the Christian beyond the Word of God. You are to reckon yourselves dead unto sin, Satan tells us, but of course you know very well that it is never actually true that you *are* dead unto sin. You will keep on sinning. When you die then will come complete deliverance, but not before. In other words, God is a liar. All Satan's wiles in the last analysis are found to be variations of this original statement of his to our first parents.

God never tells us to reckon on a lie. It is eternally true that in our position before God we are dead to sin, because we have been crucified with Christ and raised together with him. This position of ours becomes a blessed reality in actual experience as we reckon by faith, and only so long as we reckon by faith. Let Satan not rob us of our heritage by telling us it is only "positionally" that we are dead to sin. God is not thus mocking us when he tells us to "reckon" on this truth of crucifixion with Christ.

When We Reckon Self Dead to Sin

This reckoning gives us no holiness of our own. It gives no cause for boasting in our own record. It gives no uneasiness as to whether we have had this or that feeling as a witness of the Spirit.

It will be seen from these Scriptures which have been considered that every true Christian has *a measure* of victory in Christ. As Dr. Scofield has pointed out, the experience of Christians and Christian experience may be two entirely different things; for Christian experience is wholly the product of the Holy Spirit. Whatever measure of true Christian life is expressed, therefore, is the work of the Holy Spirit, and to that extent is victory by faith, even though the Christian is ignorant of the truth of the faith walk.

The Victorious Life, which is just another term for the normal "Christian Life," is simply walking moment by moment in complete faith in His perfect work.

Whether I am in victory or not at this moment is simply a question as to whether or not I am appropriating the sufficient grace of the Lord Jesus for the needs of this very moment. My glorious privilege is so to appropriate that grace, *now*, and to do it moment by moment without any breaks. For His Grace IS sufficient. His Grace is "more than enough."

CONTINUING AND GROWING IN VICTORY

A WRONG start is one of the chief causes of failure in the Victorious Life. The first secret of continuing in victory, so to speak, is to begin. Nothing can be continued unless it is begun. To see clearly that the Victorious Life is a miracle of grace, and is wholly the work of the Lord Jesus, is necessary to this right beginning. Many attempt to live the life without fully getting rid of the element of self-effort.

Having begun right, the next thing is to continue as we began. The act of surrender and faith by which we entered into victory becomes the continued attitude of the life. Failure can come only through a slip in surrender or in faith.

It is possible to abide in Christ for victory *without a break*. The Word of God says that *if* a Christian sins he is to do certain things; it never says *when* a Christian sins. It is not for us to look back over our past record to consider whether we have sinned, or to see how long we have continued without a break; but in looking into the future we must expect to be kept from sinning or we are not trusting the sufficient grace of Christ; and that means we are not at the present moment in victory.

Along with this expectation of continued victory must go the realization that at any moment we may fall into sin: "let him that thinketh he standeth take heed lest he fall," is the warning that immediately precedes the glorious promise of First Corinthians 10:13 of God's full provision for victory over every temptation.

Suppose, then, we should fall into sin after entering into the Victorious Life? *Instant and full restoration after failure* is God's plan for the Christian who sins and thus breaks the perfect abiding in the Lord. "In the moment of defeat, shout Victory!" and claim your full privileges in Christ.

But does not this make light of sin? Any other course makes light of sin. This course sees sin to be such an abominable thing in God's sight that nothing but the blood of the Lord Jesus poured out in expiation can avail to meet it. And if the blood of Jesus meets it, it is an insult to God to attempt to add anything else to that perfect atonement. Being sorry for sin for a period is an unconscious form of atonement by self effort.

The Bible—A Music Box, or a Telephone?

Without constant feeding on the Word of God and continually living in an atmosphere of prayer no one can be maintained in a life of victory. At every cost we must set our faces like a flint to get the daily quiet time with God over the Word and in prayer. This does not mean that Bible study and prayer are the secret of victory. They are not, and many are hindered from victory by supposing that their more diligent Bible study and prayer will somehow bring them into victory. *Faith* is the secret of victory. But faith is impossible without the Word, and the maintaining of faith is impossible without continually abiding in the Word of God. An infant will not live without food and air, but we would not say that food and air were the secret of that life which the Creator alone could give.

The Victorious Life gives the secret of a hunger for the Bible and prayer. The Word of God becomes literally sweeter than honey and the honeycomb, and more to be desired than gold, yea than much fine gold. Our Lord expects the Bible to be a telephone, as Dr. Charles R. Watson has said, not a music box whose tunes are familiar and stale: we take the receiver from the hook, and the Lord Jesus Christ is at the other end of the line. It is really our privilege to have a personal message from the living God to our own souls every day, and at every moment of need.

The Victorious Life and Missions

"Is not the Victorious Life rather self-centered and is there not danger of selfishness?" was asked.

"Is Christ selfish?" was the sufficient answer given to this question.

If the life of victory does not flow out in service, it is a counterfeit, and cannot be maintained. There is a reason why a passion for foreign missions will be found at the heart of all the conferences that teach the life of victory in Christ. These two are inseparable, Christ as the supply of our individual needs and Christ the sufficiency for the world's need.

Let our testimony to the Victorious Life be far more in loving, humble, unselfish service to those about us and those in the ends of the earth, than it is in the words of our lips.

Do We Grow Into Victory?

Growing in grace is one of the secrets of maintaining the life of victory; without normal growth we shall lose our victory. We do not grow *into* grace; we grow *in* it. Receiving the Victorious Life is not a matter of growth.

There are, in many cases, shorter or longer periods of growth that precede the entrance into the life of victory. So far as God is concerned, the Life is a gift and not a growth, and it may be enjoyed at once by any Christian. But the Christian may gradually come to understand what are his privileges in Christ in the matter of victory over sin. Or he may not at once get to the bottom in the surrender of life to the Lord, and God will lead him on as quickly as he will go, to the place of complete surrender and complete faith. This gradual preparation before entering fully into victory must be distinguished from "growth in grace," which goes on in a normal way only when the Christian *is* abiding in Christ for victory.

Growth in grace, in the Word of God, never means growth out of sin. There is no suggestion in the New Testament that a Christian is to grow gradually out of sin. Sin is always dealt with through the blood of Christ, and we need the Saviour every moment to keep us cleansed from sin and its defilement. But if it is the blood that cleanses us by grace we are not to eliminate sin gradually by our growth in grace.

What is "Growth in Grace"?

Growth in grace makes us more and more to conform to the likeness of our Lord Jesus. There is no perfection in his brethren on earth that can be compared to the measure of the stature of his fulness. By faith we receive the fruit of the Spirit, which is just the character of Christ produced in us by the new life of the Spirit. Every one of the nine graces which constitute the one fruit of the Spirit,—"love, joy, peace, longsuffering, kindness, goodness, faithfulness, meekness, self-control,"—belongs to the Christian who is trusting Christ for victory. But in each of these graces he is to *abound more and more*. This is true growth in grace.

One who by yielding his life to the mastery of Christ and by trusting his word, "My grace is sufficient for thee," has received the fulness of the Spirit, may know very little about the Bible, or prayer, or Christian service. Day by day he learns more of the wondrous things out of the Word, learns better how to study it and use it in personal work; day by day he learns new secrets of prayer from the Word and by the diligent practice of prayer; and gradually he becomes a more efficient and expert laborer in the harvest. This is true growth in the knowledge of the Lord.

When Invalids Grow

Growth in grace is positive, not negative. Sin is a hindrance to true growth in the spiritual life as well as in the natural life. An invalid may, indeed, grow in body, and sick Christians do grow in grace, but the growth in both cases is retarded. When the disease germs are conquered then begins normal growth. So in the Bible figure of the race toward the goal: this race is not a struggle to overcome sin, but a race which sin may greatly retard. We are counseled to lay aside every weight and the sin that clings closely about us, and run the race, looking unto Jesus. A Christian *may* run with the weights and the sin, and he is in the race, but it is not to be wondered that there are many stumbles and slow progress.

There are several passages in the New Testament which give a marvelously clear picture of this positive growth in grace, and show beautifully the distinction between the present purity of the believer and his future entire conformity to the Lord Jesus.

God's present standard of purity for his children is the purity of his only Son in whom he is well pleased. He is our Life; and apart from him we have no purity. "Every one that hath this hope set on him purifieth himself, even as he is pure" (1 John 3:3). But just before this statement of God's purpose for the present purity of his children, we read: "we know that, when he shall appear, we shall be like him; for we shall see him as he is." This is the hope set before us,—perfect conformity to the likeness of Christ. And this very hope is urged as a reason for present purity of the kind that Jesus has. Is there a contradiction here?

Tribulation as God's Molding Chisel

In Romans 3:23 we read that "all have sinned, and fall short of the glory of God." Then grace comes, we are justified in the Beloved, and in Romans 5:2 we read: "We rejoice in hope of the glory of God." But hope is always future, for "hope that is seen is not hope." This hope of the glory of God, perfect conformity to his likeness, is the same hope spoken of in First John. But in Romans five we have added light on the part that growth in grace plays. "We also rejoice in our tribulations [literally, that which presses down]: knowing that tribulation worketh stedfastness, [literally, that which holds up under the load]; and stedfastness, approvedness [literally, passing the examination or the test]; and approvedness, hope [hope of the glory of God, or the character of God]. Then follows this remarkable statement: "and hope putteth not to shame."

A future hope will always put to shame if there is no present guarantee that the hope will be realized. If I announce that a certain rich man is to give me a fortune of ten million dollars ten years hence, the hope of this wealth will put to shame if there is nothing to show that the millionaire will keep his word. My friends are likely to say, "We shall wait and see." But if the millionaire gives me as an earnest of the expected inheritance a check for half a million dollars, my hope does not put me to shame.

Now notice what follows God's statement that this hope of his glory puts not to shame: "because the love of God hath been shed abroad in our hearts through the Holy Spirit which was given unto us." The perfect guarantee of my *future* likeness to the Lord Jesus is the miracle of my *present* likeness to him. The love of God shed abroad in my heart makes me like Jesus. The love of God shed abroad keeps out hatred and all other manifestations of self, so long as the Spirit is in control and can express his fruit. The Holy Spirit is the payment down of this future glory. The Holy Spirit *hath been given* unto us, not will be; this is not a future hope. The Holy Spirit is our earnest. "In whom, having also believed, ye were sealed with the Holy Spirit of promise, which is an earnest of our inheritance" (Eph. 1:13, 14).

Make Use of Your "Earnest"!

In rejoicing in that glorious hope of what is to be brought to us at the appearing of the Lord Jesus, let us take care not to despise the present provision for victory and purity in the Holy Spirit. We long for the redemption of our bodies, that we may be clothed upon with that tabernacle which is from heaven, "that what is mortal may be swallowed up of life," and that we may have a body like his glorious body; but meanwhile we have the firstfruits of the Spirit, and we rejoice in the tribulations and all the things this body endures because it works out in that growth which gives more and more of his own character (Rom. 8:23-26; 2 Cor. 5:1-5).

These passages in Romans and Second Corinthians just quoted make it clear that the future hope refers particularly to the redemption of our bodies, when we shall have a body like to the body of his glory. Every Christian will receive this body and be conformed to his likeness; for this, as is every part of our redemption, is all of grace. But while all Christians will share the purity and the glory, not all Christians will have the same *measure* of glory. "There is one glory of the sun, and another glory of the moon, and another glory of the stars; for one star differeth from another star in glory. So also is the resurrection of the dead" (1 Cor. 15:41, 42). The enduring of tribulation, the working out of stedfastness and approvedness,—growth in grace,—will undoubtedly determine the degree of glory in that resurrection body.

The Key-Verse on Growth in Grace

Probably no better key-verse on growth in grace can be found than Second Corinthians 3:18, and in that verse is gathered up the messages of these other passages that have been considered: "But we all, with unveiled face beholding as in a mirror the glory of the Lord, are transformed into the same image from glory to glory, even as from the Lord the Spirit." As we look unto Jesus, and grow in his knowledge and grace, we are changed, as one scholar has translated it, "from one degree of glory to another degree of glory."

As we get to know the Lord Jesus better and better, sin becomes more horrible to us; we see its true character. This does not mean that we become worse sinners, for we are growing from one degree of glory to another. But we appreciate more and more what sinners we were by nature, apart from grace; we see the depravity that follows sin, and we exalt the grace of the Lord Jesus Christ which has saved and is saving us from such sin and corruption.

The margin of Second Corinthians 3:18 adds a final glorious touch: instead of "beholding as in a mirror" there is the translation which many believe more accurate, "reflecting as in a mirror the glory of the Lord." It is ours to behold and then to reflect. Do they see Jesus in us? It is "Christ in you, the hope of glory" (Col. 1:27). He himself is the secret of growth in grace, as of all else.

CAN MAN BE FREE FROM SIN?

"HOW can I be free from sin?" is the question that in one form or another is troubling the heart of many a true child of God. But before we ask "How?" the other query rises, "*Can* I be free from sin?" and if not completely in this life, "How far may I be free?"

As is to be expected, the teaching of the Word of God on the sin question is simple, direct and unequivocal. But there are a number of misconceptions that have served to confuse the minds of many earnest seekers after the truth.

One of the best tests of the truth of our view of sin is the results in experience. It is, however, a blessed fact that one may have an experience that is infinitely better than the theory he holds regarding sin.

That sinning is inevitable for the Christian,—

That sinning is an accident, not the choice of a free moral agent,—

That sinning is an incident, not a preventable tragedy,—

That Christians may reach in this life a state in which they cannot sin, or where they are not subject to temptation,—

These are some of the contradictions of God's revealed truth which result in keeping Christians from having complete liberty in Christ and freedom from sinning.

Back of the question, how far may we be free from sin is the further problem, "What is sin?" and it is in answering this question that we may fall into a fundamental misconception which leaves us confused when reading the plain statements of Scripture. Many a supposed difference among Christians regarding freedom from sinning rests back in a difference in their definition of "sinning." But this is far more serious than a mere difference in the definition of a word, which might be passed over as unimportant. For, as we shall see, if our use of the word "sinning" differs from that which God means by sin, there is sure to result a confusion which will affect our experience in the matter of deliverance from sin.

There is substantial agreement that Christians should be, and may be, free from dishonesty, lying, stealing, jealousy, strife, bitterness, evil speaking, fornication, covetousness, and a thousand other sins that might be named. Also it is agreed that it is not for Christians to grow out of such sins, nor to get rid of them gradually, but to put them off as wholly inconsistent with the Christian walk. How complete is the list of such sins that a Christian may be free from just now? Or to put the question in another form, how much sin is it necessary for a Christian to have?

"But," some one asks, "is not everything that falls short of God's absolute standard of perfection sin?" Our purpose in this study is intensely practical, and so it is not the intention to enter into a full discussion of theological terms. It may be suggested in passing that many who use such an expression as "God's absolute standard of perfection," would find great difficulty in explaining just what they mean. But we may here get at the problem as it presents itself in experience. All are agreed that there is no possibility of perfection of attainment in this body, meaning by such perfection an absence of all error or mistake in everything that is done. We may go further and say that by this standard of "perfection" every act falls short, and every moment of life is compassed with infirmity. If this kind of "falling short" is sin, then there can be full agreement that there is no such thing as freedom from sinning in this body. (It would not be entirely accurate to say, "if this imperfection is sin," for "perfection," like all words—and everything else human—is imperfect and relative and takes its meaning from the thought in the mind of the user.)

Is such falling short sinning? Or to reduce the question to practical everyday experience, "Is every act of the Christian sinful, as well as every word and thought?"

Three Bible teachers met together on one occasion to discuss the sin question; before they began their conference one of them suggested that they have prayer, and he led in petition for their guidance and blessing. This brother, a theological professor and a Christian noted for his holy living, contended that everything a Christian did was of necessity tainted with sin because it fell short of "perfection."

"Doctor," one of the others asked, "is there not a difference between the sin we committed when we prayed together at the beginning of our conference and the sin I should commit if I were critical or bitter against you?"

"Yes, there is a difference," he replied (answering according to Scripture and his common sense), "but" (answering according to his theory) "it is a very dangerous thing to make distinctions between sins."

It is a disastrous thing *not* to make distinction between these two things. With one stroke we would blot out the difference between light and darkness if we class together the act of a Christian who with a heart full of love pours out his petition in imperfect words for some needy one, and the act of a man who with his heart full of hate runs a dagger through the heart of that same needy one. There is the same infinity of difference between this "imperfect" prayer and the critical or unloving attitude that the praying Christian might later fall into.

Turning from men's reasonings regarding sin to the Word of God, we find these plain statements:

"My little children, these things write I unto you, that ye may not sin" (1 John 2:1).

Something had been written, then, which revealed the secret of keeping from sin as a present, practical experience for the child of God.

"What shall we say then? Shall we continue in sin, that grace may abound?" (Rom. 6:1.)

"What then? shall we sin, because we are not under law, but under grace?" (Rom. 6:15.)

God's answer to both these questions, which is just one question put in two ways, is the same: a strong, emphatic negative—"God forbid."

There can be little question in the minds of any that what John means by sinning in this first letter of his, and what Paul means by sinning in Romans six, is something that a Christian should not and need not do. He may be kept from sinning, in this meaning of the word.

It may well be asked, what other meaning of the word is there? If we start out with the conception of sinning that makes every act of a Christian to be tainted with sin, do not the Scriptures become a real puzzle in their positive statements about keeping from sin? This supposed difficulty has given rise to an attempted distinction between "conscious" and "unconscious" sinning. Those who use these terms do not always have the same distinction in mind, but some refer to this falling short of "perfection" as "unconscious sinning," adding that such sin needs cleansing but involves no guilt.

But *all sin involves guilt.* God cannot do other than condemn sin, whether in the Christian or in the unbeliever. Moreover, neither in First John, nor in Romans six, nor anywhere in the New Testament is there distinction made between "conscious" and "unconscious" sinning, or "known" and "unknown" sins. These distinctions between sins are made by men with the implication that we may be kept free from one kind of sinning but not from the other. Does not this make void the word of God by our traditions? For God says, through John, "My little children, these things write I unto you, *that ye may not sin.*"

We shall avoid all such difficulties if we rid ourselves of the notion that the sinfulness or the righteousness of a man's act is to be judged by some outside standard. God's measure is an inside standard. Sin can never be discovered in the act, but in the motive of the heart of the man who performs the act. Two men go into a restaurant and hang up their overcoats. Two other men in the restaurant take these overcoats with them when they go out. One man has stolen an overcoat. The other man has taken it by mistake, thinking he had brought his own overcoat with him, and is much distressed when he finds he has another man's coat. But meanwhile both men have lost their coats. Nothing can be determined as to whether sin is involved until you get to the heart of the men who took the coats. One man sinned. The other man surely came short of that perfect outward standard of action, and he should not have been so thoughtless as to take the coat. The experience will doubtless make him more careful in the future in avoiding such a mistake. But he did not sin. And if our theory makes it necessary for us to say that he sinned, then we have blotted out all moral distinctions, and there is an end of urging men to come out of darkness into light.

Since sin is in the motive of the heart, it becomes clear why a man who is out of Christ is sinning all the time, in thought, word and deed. He may do many moral things and live on a high plane judged by man's standard, but he is incapable of God's righteousness. Only the love of God shed abroad in the heart through the Holy Spirit can make righteousness possible. A natural, unsaved man cannot please God in anything that he does. That is why he must be born again before he is capable of goodness. When he is saved he may love God with his whole heart, and then he can and does please God. And let us remember that no man can please God with sinning, whatever adjective is prefixed.

Another fruitful source of confusion in studying the Scripture teachings regarding sin is the taking of Bible statements concerning man in his natural state and applying them to the new creature in Christ Jesus.

"There is none righteous, no, not one" (Rom. 3:10).

"There is none that doeth good, no, not so much as one" (Rom. 3:12).

"All have sinned, and fall short of the glory of God" (Rom. 3:23).

"In thy sight no man living is righteous" (Ps. 143:2).

These statements are used in Scripture to describe the condition of all men outside of Jesus Christ the Saviour. To wrest these words from their connection and apply them to saved men to prove that they are not righteous and that they continually are coming short of the glory of God, is to take all meaning and significance out of the language of Scripture. It is because this is our natural state that we need a Saviour. When He saves us, are we left in the same state? Some have carried this strange use of the words of Scripture to the extent of believing (or thinking that they believe) that Paul considered himself still the chief of sinners after he was saved. He speaks of himself as the chief of sinners for the very purpose of showing the greatness of the grace of the Saviour which availed to save the chief of sinners, and that grace was not found vain. But what would we say of a Saviour whose grace abounded in such a way as still to leave Saul the chief of sinners? That is not Paul's Saviour, and that is not the way Christ's grace operates even in the lives of those true Christians who think they believe themselves still to be unrighteous sinners.

Perhaps the Scripture that has suffered most from this method of lifting it out from its environment is First John, one, eight: "If we say that we have no sin, we deceive ourselves, and the truth is not in us." A passage which was written for the express purpose of giving the children of God the glad tidings that they need not sin, and pointing out God's provision for keeping them walking in the light, has somehow become for many a stumbling block which keeps them in darkness.

Now whatever John, one, eight means it must be in accord with the later word that these things he was writing that we may not sin. "And if any man sin, we have an Advocate." "*If any sin.*" That means there is a possibility of *not sinning*, as well as the admitted possibility of sinning. He does not say "*When* a Christian sins," which would make sin inevitable. Now if a Christian were sinning all the time, this word of assurance against sinning, and also the word of comfort and assurance for the Christian who has been overtaken in a fault would be robbed of all meaning. First John, one, eight, therefore, cannot mean that Christians are sinning continually, or if they are, the next verses urge them to get out of that condition.

The literal rendering of this verse is, "If we say that we have not sin," or "If we say that we do not have sin." The negative is an adverb, not an adjective. The ordinary renderings, "If we say that we have *no* sin," might encourage the assumption that the Apostle was speaking of degrees of sin and warning against the thought of being free from all sin. But sin is not something that can be divided; if there is sin, there is sin, and it is not here a question of more or less sin.

It will help also to remember that there is no independent First John, one, eight in the Word. This sentence is part of a closely woven argument running from the fifth verse of the first chapter to the sixth verse of the second chapter. He is talking of fellowship with God, which is an absolute thing in the sense that we either have perfect fellowship or we do not have perfect fellowship, just as a man wants perfect fellowship with his wife though the fellowship deepens and becomes richer as the days go on. There is but one thing that can break this fellowship with God, John says, and that is sin. For God is light and in Him is no darkness, and the man that has fellowship must walk in the light. Therefore man needs to be cleansed from sin so that he may walk in the light, having fellowship. There were some in his day, as in ours, who were saying that they had fellowship, though they were walking in darkness. If we say that, we lie. But if we admit that we cannot have fellowship and be in darkness, and are cleansed from sin in the blood of Christ, then we may walk in the light. If we say that we do not have sin, and therefore do not need this cleansing, we deceive ourselves. But if we are not deceived in this way and confess our sins, he is faithful and righteous to forgive us and to cleanse us from all unrighteousness, so that we may walk in the light. If we say, as they were saying in his day, that we have not sinned, we make God a liar, for he has said that all men have sinned and come short of the glory of God, and therefore need a Saviour. John is writing all of this for the purpose of keeping these Christians from sinning, not for the purpose of explaining to them that they must be sinning continually while they are walking in the light. Sin breaks the fellowship, and before a man sins he must step out of that light. This is the message of the whole of First John. He may confess and be cleansed and restored to the fellowship, walking in the light.

But was not John referring to Christians when he said "we"? Let us ask if John meant that he and other Christians would say that they had fellowship with God when they were walking in the darkness; or would he and others say that they had not sinned, and thus make God a liar? The "we," of course, is used in the same sense as, "If *any one* says that he has fellowship with him." It is the use of the first personal pronoun that we ourselves continually make in stating universal truths. Some have even brought consternation to rescue mission workers by telling them never to use First John, one, nine for sinners, because the "we" refers to Christians, and God is "faithful and just" to forgive Christians, because they are under the covenant, while it is of his mercy that he forgives sinners. But "he is the propitiation for our sins; and not for ours only, but *also for the whole world*," and since God has given Christ to die for the world, it is of his righteousness and justice to forgive every sinner the instant he turns to the Saviour. This is not to say that it is not also of his mercy, but as one has suggested it is mercy from start to finish, for the Christian as well as the sinner. The rescue mission workers and other soul winners may go on using this verse with a clear conscience, for God will honor it both for sinners, and for Christians when they act like sinners, and need to confess and be forgiven.

In *The Sunday School Times* there was published recently a remarkable testimony of one who was saved from Christian Science, and the verse that brought conviction was First John, one, eight. "Why, that is just what I have been doing," this woman said in amazement to herself one time when she read this verse. "I have been saying that I have no sin, and I am deceived. I need a Saviour." This is the Spirit's use of that passage; if it refers to Christians who have confessed their sins and have accepted the Saviour and been cleansed from sin, there can remain in it no convicting power for the one who has not confessed.

These brief suggestions upon this passage are given with the thought of provoking further study, and the reader may still feel strongly that First John, one, eight refers to Christians, whatever their spiritual state may be. Let us grant that it does, and the Christian then is confessing to God and to men, "I have sin." Putting aside the difficulty of understanding how it is possible for me to be without condemnation for the sin, or how it is possible for me to walk in the light in fellowship with God while I have this sin, let us face this simple question, "When am I going to get rid of this sin?"

There are at least seven theories that have been suggested to answer this question, and to get rid of the "root of sin" which it is supposed John is dealing with when he says, "If we say that we have not sin, we deceive ourselves." All are agreed that without holiness no man shall see God, and that this means actual holiness; and therefore all who hold these different theories are agreed that this root of sin referred to by John must be gotten out, or eradicated.

The first theory is *gradual eradication after death*, or gradual purification, for which a place called purgatory is provided (by the theology, not by the Lord). This theory of course is a matter of works from start to finish, and perhaps no reader of these pages would entertain it.

The second is *gradual eradication during life, with the completion of the process at death*. In this theory the process during life makes no real progress toward the consummation at death since all equally need the work at death, whatever the degree of eradication during life.

The third is *increasing counteraction during life, with eradication at death*. That is, the evil is not eradicated gradually during life but is counteracted increasingly by the power of God, while remaining till its removal at death.

The fourth is *eradication at death*. That is, the evil is unaffected during life, and awaits death for its removal.

The fifth is *eradication at the coming of Christ*. But if we die we enter into the presence of His holiness and need purity before this event.

Few maintain this theory, except those who go the length of identifying the root of sin with the physical body or with the blood, thus making sin inhere in matter. This assumption is also needed to give support to the second, third and fourth theories, for the only change that, takes place at death is the separation of the spirit from the body.

The sixth is *eradication before death*, requiring a second work of grace, subsequent to regeneration.

The seventh is *eradication at the moment of regeneration*, which perhaps few in our day hold, though it has been earnestly contended for in other days.

All of these eradication theories, with the exception of the last, make necessary a second work of grace subsequent to regeneration. They mean that God has to do something else to free a man from sin after he is cleansed, by faith, in the blood of Christ, and made a new creature by the operation of the Holy Spirit. For manifestly, if a Christian must say, "I have sin," he must get rid of that sin, and it must be done at one of three times: before death, at death, or after death. Is there a line of Scripture that gives support to any one of these six theories of a second work of grace, or of the theory of eradication at the first work of grace?

All of these theories rest upon the assumption that there is a "root of sin" *in* a man, in a mechanical, material sense, and that from this root sin springs.

The Scripture testimony is that *the man himself is the root of sin.* Sin springs from *him.* Our Lord said that out of the heart proceed evil thoughts and deeds that defile the man. He was not speaking of the heart as a physical or spiritual entity *in the man*, but showing the Pharisees that righteousness or evil did not consist in the outward acts or observances, but proceeded *from the man himself.* For the heart is the man.

This natural man, who is himself the root of his sin, must be born again. It is the man himself who is born again, made a new creature in Christ Jesus. The heart, that is, the man himself, is purified by faith, through the miracle work of the Holy Spirit. This new man, who in the moment of regeneration has the fruit of the Spirit, his heart filled with love, continues to have victory in Christ as he continues to abide in Christ. "As therefore ye received Christ Jesus the Lord, so walk in him" (Col. 2:6). This is God's plan. It is because Christians have not continued so walking, or perhaps because they have not known clearly and fully the normal New Testament experience that should result from "receiving" Christ Jesus, that there is need of a crisis in the life, a decision to get back where we belong in the place of abiding.

But why is it possible for this new creature to sin after he has so received Christ? It has been assumed that there must be some root of sin in the Christian that makes it possible for him to sin. It is strange that this should be thought a necessity when we know that Satan sinned, and Adam sinned, when they were sinless and had never been tainted with any impurity. If it were *not* possible for this new creature to sin, he would be a machine; his very humanity would need to be destroyed. If we accept as the alternative of this kind of Christian a Christian who is provided with something in him which causes the sin, we arrive at exactly the same conclusion with this difference: we have a machine which cannot do anything except sin. Let it be understood clearly that if a man in this body and in this life in the midst of temptation is not able to sin then he is not able to be good. He can sin for the same reason that he can be good, because he is a free moral agent. That is the way God made him, and it is of the essence of his humanity. Everywhere in Scripture the Christian is appealed to as one who is responsible to choose. The reason that a Christian can sin is because he still has his free will. And when he sins, it is not a root of sin in him that sins. It is he who sins.

That first sin (which need not occur) after a man is made a new creature in Christ, or after he has understood and taken Christ as his Victory, is always a tragedy. Sin should always be a tragedy. It is not an accident nor an incident. But if the man is not responsible, but has something in him that makes sin necessary, then he cannot regard sin as a preventable tragedy.

But it is not possible for God to sin, and yet he can be good. Here we come to the heart of our confusion regarding a Christian's goodness. God not only can be good, He himself *is goodness*. He is holy in a way that no man ever was or ever can be. For man's holiness is never absolute in this sense, but always relative. Not relative in the sense that sin must be present, but relative because of the moment by moment relationship with God, the Holy One. Therefore for the Christian to be kept from sinning he must abide in Christ, and he cannot do other than sin if left to himself. At the root of all these eradication theories lies the assumption that man is to be made independently holy. But man is a dependent creature. This is of the essence of humanity, altogether apart from sin. Utter dependence on his creator and his Saviour (and the Saviour is the creator of the new life) is the only safety for the child of God. There is indeed no room for boasting nor for looking to self when we learn God's wondrous plan of salvation by grace.

Two Christian workers were talking together at the lunch table about the question of what happened to a man when he is saved. One of the brethren pointed to the granulated sugar in the bowl as representing him as a lost man. He then took a spoon as representing the divine life imparted in conversion, stuck it into the sugar, and said: "This represents my new nature, and the sugar is still the same corrupt nature. But I am in Christ as the sugar is in the bowl." In other words Christ is enclosing a mass of corruption with a righteous spark injected into it.

Another Christian worker, representing what Christ did in saving him, drew his coat about him so as to cover up his white vest, and said that in just this way God clothes us with Christ's righteousness, while we remain a mass of corruption beneath.

Still another, putting these illustrations into theological terms, said: "God imputes the righteousness of Christ to me in exactly the same way as he imputes my sin to Christ. So that when God looks at me he sees the righteousness of Christ, just as when he looks at Jesus he sees my sin." The implication is that righteousness touches me in just the way that sin touches Christ, namely, it is as far from me as the east is from the west.

These brethren are all true children of God, washed in the precious blood of Christ. Fortunately they were not telling the truth about themselves; more seriously they were maligning the Saviour, and while the intellectual confusion may not keep them from victory in their own lives it serves to entangle many an earnest seeker. And this sort of handling of God's word is what has furnished the enemies of the Gospel of grace their chief weapons in attack. These statements, if they are taken at their face value, constitute as complete a denial of the God and Father of our Lord and Saviour Jesus Christ as Mrs. Eddy's philosophy of the denial of sin and the Saviour.

As Luther roused the Church by the battle cry of "Justification by Faith," let the complete truth of the complete Gospel be sounded to-day in the cry of "Salvation by Faith." For "it is of faith, that it may be according to Grace" (Rom. 4:16). God never justifies a sinner without saving him. That is, he does not call a man righteous without making him righteous. If he did, God would be in the place of the man whom James condemns, who says to the brother or sister naked and in need of daily food: "Go in peace, be ye warmed and filled," yet gives them not the things needful to the body. "What doth it profit?" James asks. "Even so faith, if it have not works, is dead in itself" (Jas. 2:15-17).

Even so would the calling a man righteous without making him righteous be useless for the soul that is naked and destitute of righteousness. Justification, in the sense of "declaring righteous," is dead apart from the miracle of cleansing and regeneration which *makes righteous*. And we need righteousness, just as the naked and hungry man needs clothing and food, *now in this life*. There is no hope held out for any future provision of freeing from sin. There is still a part of our redemption from sin and its results that is future, but very distinctly are we told that this concerns the redemption of our body, not the purifying of the soul. (Using purifying in its negative meaning of cleansing from impurity. For we must remember that there is a positive, progressive, and increasing work in conforming us to the likeness of Christ which is quite distinct from this matter of cleansing, which is always absolute; we are either cleansed or we are not cleansed from sin.)

The works that James insists on as a proof that the faith is real faith, are possible only for the new creature in Christ, who is producing the fruit of the Spirit as he abides in Christ, the fruit which is the righteousness of Christ made real in experience, and abounding more and more as we grow in grace (not into grace), and the knowledge of our Lord and Saviour Jesus Christ.

Not a half salvation of "justification by faith" to take care of the past only of our sins, but let our watchword be a complete salvation of "CHRIST BY

FAITH." For it is Christ that saves from sin, who makes a new creation with old things put away, and who provides a way of abiding in that freedom, walking in joy and peace and victory, just as we received Him in freedom.

"If, therefore, the Son shall make you free, ye shall be free indeed."

"Being made free from sin, ye became servants of righteousness."

"Now being made free from sin and become servants of God, ye have your fruit unto sanctification."

"For freedom did Christ set us free: Stand fast therefore, and be not entangled again in a yoke of bondage."

THE HOLY SPIRIT

IF the Victorious Life is "the life that is Christ," lived in the power of the risen Christ dwelling in the heart, what is the work of the Holy Spirit in such a life? Are Christians who pray for, or seek, the "fullness of the Spirit," or the "baptism of the Spirit" or the "receiving of the Spirit," asking for something different from the life of victory in Christ?

The answer to such questions reveals the beautiful unity of God's plan of salvation, in which each Person of the Godhead has His perfect work but in which our Lord Jesus Christ has ever the pre-eminence till the work of salvation is completed. We may approach the truth from teaching concerning the Holy Spirit, but it is Christ who will be exalted. Or we may experience resurrection life through learning of the truth concerning the indwelling Christ, but it is the Holy Spirit who makes possible that experience in the life.

The Holy Spirit is God. If we start with this fact, and stay with it, we shall be saved from much confusion as to the Holy Spirit's office. If he is God, we cannot limit Him, and we cannot confine Him to this or that manifestation of His power.

The Holy Spirit is not merely a manifestation of God; He *is* God. And one Person of the trinity is never present without the others. While the Holy Spirit has a distinct work in the believer, this work is never disassociated from the other Persons in the Godhead. The Father and the Son and the Spirit all dwell with us (John 14:17, 23; 1 Cor. 6:19; 2 Cor. 13:5).

The Holy Spirit is a Person. We are not to seek a quantitative appropriation of a certain amount of the Spirit of God, perhaps comparing the amount we have with that which we think others have, but rather to receive God the Holy Spirit, who is a Person. But this truth of His personality is to be kept in balance by the companion truth that He is God, and in conceiving Him as a person we must not put the limitations of human personality upon God, as though He could only indwell one person at a time, or as though one person or any number of persons could exhaustively contain Him.

What is the work of God the Holy Spirit in this age? We know that we are born again by the power of the Spirit, and the Holy Spirit is in every child of God (John 1:12, 13; John 3:5, 6; Rom. 8:9, last clause; 1 Cor. 6-19).

If the Holy Spirit is in every child of God, what result does this have in the life? What is His work in the believer? Is it the same for each believer? In what sense did the Holy Spirit come at Pentecost, and in what sense is he here in a different way from His manifestation before Pentecost?

It is in answering such questions that we are in danger of building up a doctrine from experience rather than from the Word.

A Bible teacher who has been mightily used in soul-winning and in stimulating other Christians to this work, dates his great success from the time when he learned that the Holy Spirit was the secret of power in service; he lacked the power, saw the need, asked for the fulness of the Holy Spirit, by faith believed that God had granted his desire, went out boldly with no reference to feeling and counted upon the fact of the Holy Spirit's work as he gave the message to men. The results were marvelous, and continued to be as day by day he counted upon this enduement of the Spirit. Along with this experience came the inevitable longing to share it with others, for he knew that any Christian might do as he had done; the blessed result was that many Christians through him were led into this new life of service. It was natural that this mighty man of God should take his true and Scriptural experience and build around it his doctrine of the Holy Spirit and His work for believers, interpreting the Scriptures by the experience. So he developed an inclusive doctrinal teaching that the baptism of the Holy Spirit at Pentecost, and to-day in the life of the individual believer, is for power in service, the evidence of the work being the results in witnessing.

Another Christian worker had a longing for heart purity and a life free from any feeling of condemnation because everything was not pleasing to God. He heard a testimony from a brother who had been in a like state and had learned that it was not by effort or struggle or trying that he was to get peace and purity, but by the work of God through the Holy Spirit coming into or upon the believer and purifying the heart. As the first mentioned brother did, he asked God for this gift and then by faith believed that his prayer was answered. The result was an amazing transformation, a life of joy and liberty which was such a miracle revelation and so different from the average Christian experience that many came to him asking for the secret. He told them what had happened, and he too proceeded to put together his doctrine of the Holy Spirit and taught that every Christian who was born of the Spirit needed to seek as a second work the baptism of the Holy Spirit to bring purity of heart.

There is no question that these brethren experienced the gracious power of the Holy Spirit. But they did not accurately relate those experiences to the teachings of the Word.

In John 7:39 is suggested what the fundamental, primary work of the Holy Spirit was to be, and why He was able to come into the world in a new way at Pentecost. After our Lord, in the last great day of the feast, cried, "If any man thirst, let him come unto Me and drink. He that believeth on Me, as the Scripture hath said, from within him shall flow rivers of living water," the apostle explains, "But this spake he of the Spirit, which they that believed on him were to receive for the Spirit was not yet given; because Jesus was not yet glorified."

The Spirit was to be given at Pentecost in a way in which He was not given before. And it is expressly stated that the one thing needed before His being thus given was the glorifying of the Son of man.

Link this with our Lord's word in John 16:13, 14 and we have clearly revealed the connection between the glorifying of the Son of man and the work of the Spirit: "He (the Holy Spirit) shall not speak for himself.... He shall glorify me."

This is His specific work, to glorify Jesus. But how?

"Nevertheless I tell you the truth: It is expedient for you that I go away, for if I go not away, the Comforter will not come unto you; but if I go, I will send him unto you. And he, when he is come, will convict the world in respect of sin, and of righteousness, and of judgment: of sin, because they believe not on me; of righteousness, because I go to the Father, and ye behold me no more; of judgment, because the Prince of this world hath been judged" (John 16:7-11).

How is the Holy Spirit to convict the world of sin, of righteousness, of judgment? Notice it is conviction of one sin, not many, the one sin of rejecting the Saviour. It is one righteousness, the righteousness that Christ is. It is one judgment, the past judgment upon Satan, the completed victory over our great Adversary won by Christ.

In the words "ye behold me no more," we have the key to the marvelous truth of this revelation concerning the Holy Spirit. The only example the world had of God's righteousness (which is the only kind of righteousness there is,) was the Lord Jesus Christ, the Son of Man. When He goes to the Father how is the world to know what righteousness is? for it can behold the righteous one no more. They cannot know it by reading about it. There is one way, and one way only to reveal righteousness, that is in a human being living a righteous life. To secure this Jesus Christ the righteous One must be manifest in the life. "They see me no more. They must know righteousness by looking at *you*. I have been the light of the world while in it. Now you, having become sons of light, are to be the light of the world" (John 12:23, 31, 35, 36; John 17:1, 22).

This is how the Holy Spirit glorifies Christ, by crowning Him Lord in the life, and manifesting the Son of man in each of His brethren. The world is convicted of sin by seeing the meaning of rejecting the Saviour as revealed in the man who accepts Him. The world is convicted of righteousness, and the difference between God's righteousness and man's morality, by seeing a righteous man. The world is convicted of the judgment of the prince of this world by seeing a life set free from the power of Satan.

This is why the disciples had to wait at Pentecost, not wait to get themselves into a certain receptive spiritual state, but wait till the Son of man was glorified and the Holy Spirit was sent forth. They did not need further knowledge of the facts about Christ the Saviour. But before they became witnesses to Jesus Christ, they themselves must become living messages, living witnesses, by having Jesus Christ revealed *in them*. This is what the Holy Spirit did, and this is what would be impossible without the Holy Spirit given in this new way.

Some one has well said that the Holy Spirit is for the servant, rather than for the service. The service and the life is the normal outflow when the servant, the man himself, has been filled with the Holy Spirit.

The fulness of the Spirit, this new work of the Spirit for the believer, is just the Christ life manifested in the believer. This is the fruit of the Spirit, "love, joy, peace, longsuffering, kindness, goodness, faithfulness, meekness, self-control" (Gal. 5:22, 23). This is the love of God shed abroad in our hearts through the Holy Spirit given unto us (Rom. 5:5). This is the earnest of our inheritance—the hope of glory that puts not to shame (Eph. 1:13, 14; Rom. 5:1, 5). This is the transforming power for growth in grace (2 Cor. 3:18). This is the thirteenth of First Corinthians made real in our experience, the love which is the fulfilling of the law.

The Holy Spirit convicts and comforts. He convicts the world, and also the believer when he walks after the world. He comforts the saints, and we have noted something of what this means. The Holy Spirit makes possible the life of victory in Christ. The fulness of the Spirit, walking in the Spirit, the Spirit indwelling the life (that is, controlling it), are all other ways of saying, the life that is Christ, the Victorious Life, the life kept from sinning, the Christ-controlled life.

The Holy Spirit gives distinct gifts for worship and service, he works miracles, he does many things for the believer. But these things which he does for different believers, dividing to each severally even as He will, must be kept distinct from the one central purpose which is the same for every believer, namely the manifesting of Christ in the life (Gal. 3:5; 1 Cor. 12 to 14; Eph. 4:14-16).

And the one proof that Christ is not manifested, is *sin*. Thus victory over sin is central in the work of the Spirit in our salvation.

We have asked and briefly answered two questions concerning the Holy Spirit: "Who is He, and what does He do?" "Who has Him, and what do they do?" There remains a third question, the answer to which determines whether His miracle working power shall be available in present experience: "Has He me?"

The Holy Spirit may be in a believer, and yet not controlling the life. This is the meaning of the exhortation to Christians in Ephesians 5:18: "Be filled with the Spirit." These believers were born of the Spirit and sealed with the Spirit (Eph. 1:13), yet there was the possibility of their not being filled with the Spirit. This is the meaning of the charge, "Walk by the Spirit, and ye shall not fulfil the lust of the flesh" (Gal 5:6). There was a possibility of walking after the flesh. So in Romans 8:4 Paul declares that the righteous requirement of the law is "fulfilled in us, who walk not after the flesh, but after the Spirit." This is the life of victory, lived in the power of the Spirit. And this is the life which a believer may effectually hinder by his own will in keeping from yielding to the control of the Spirit, whose control means the manifesting of Christ.

The Christian who is ready to yield completely to Christ may in the very moment of yielding trust Christ for the fulness of the Spirit, knowing that His fruit in life and service is now being produced. The simple condition of surrender and faith for victory is what gives the Holy Spirit sway in the life.

What relation has such a crisis of the fulness of the Spirit of regeneration? Is it a crisis that necessarily must follow the crisis of the new birth? The answer is clearly given in Galatians 5:25. "If we live by the Spirit, by the Spirit let us also walk." If we have eternal life by the miracle work of the Holy Spirit, by that same miracle power let us live our daily lives moment by moment. There would not need to be a crisis after conversion if we stayed in the place of abiding where we started, in full surrender and trust.

The message of Galatians 5:25, in terms of the Holy Spirit's work, is precisely the message of Colossians 2:6 in terms of Christ: "As ye received Christ Jesus the Lord, so walk in him." In normal regeneration the child of God is not only born of the Spirit, but filled with the Spirit. Thousands testify that in that moment their heart was filled with love, the fruit of the Spirit was produced all at once in the life. God's plan is that such a life should abide in Christ, walking in the Spirit. Only one thing can interrupt such abiding and that is assertion of self, which is sin, or walking after the flesh. It is because sin has entered that Christians need the crisis to get back to where they were, or where they might have been, in the moment of regeneration.

It is Jesus the Baptist who baptizes with the Holy Spirit those who believe in Him, the Saviour. And it is Jesus, the Son of man, who is glorified by the Holy Spirit as He manifests Him in the life yielded to His control.

Have thine own way, Lord. Have thine own way.

Hold o'er my being absolute sway.

Fill with thy Spirit, till all shall see

    Christ only, always, living in me.

Milton Keynes UK
Ingram Content Group UK Ltd.
UKHW030911151124
451262UK00006B/830